Congressional
Research
Service

Unfunded Mandates Reform Act: History, Impact, and Issues

Robert Jay Dilger
Senior Specialist in American National Government

Richard S. Beth
Specialist on Congress and the Legislative Process

October 22, 2012

Congressional Research Service

7-5700

www.crs.gov

R40957

CRS Report for Congress

Prepared for Members and Committees of Congress

Summary

The Unfunded Mandates Reform Act of 1995 (UMRA) culminated years of effort by state and local government officials and business interests to control, if not eliminate, the imposition of unfunded intergovernmental and private-sector federal mandates. Advocates argued the statute was needed to forestall federal legislation and regulations that imposed obligations on state and local governments or businesses that resulted in higher costs and inefficiencies. Opponents argued that federal mandates may be necessary to achieve national objectives in areas where voluntary action by state and local governments and business failed to achieve desired results.

UMRA provides a framework for the Congressional Budget Office (CBO) to estimate the direct costs of mandates in legislative proposals to state and local governments and to the private sector, and for issuing agencies to estimate the direct costs of mandates in proposed regulations to regulated entities. Aside from these informational requirements, UMRA controls the imposition of mandates only through a procedural mechanism allowing Congress to decline to consider unfunded intergovernmental mandates in proposed legislation if they are estimated to cost more than specified threshold amounts. UMRA applies to any provision in legislation, statute, or regulation that would impose an enforceable duty upon state and local governments or the private sector. It does not apply to conditions of federal assistance; duties stemming from participation in voluntary federal programs; rules issued by independent regulatory agencies; rules issued without a general notice of proposed rulemaking; and rules and legislative provisions that cover individual constitutional rights, discrimination, emergency assistance, grant accounting and auditing procedures, national security, treaty obligations, and certain elements of Social Security.

State and local government officials argue that UMRA has restrained the growth of unfunded federal mandates, but that its coverage should be broadened, with special consideration given to including conditions of federal financial assistance. Reflecting these views, H.R. 373, the Unfunded Mandates Information and Transparency Act of 2011 (as amended), and H.R. 4078, the Red Tape Reduction and Small Business Job Creation Act: Title IV, the Unfunded Mandates Information and Transparency Act of 2012, which was passed by the House on July 26, 2012, would, among other things, broaden UMRA's coverage to include assessments of indirect costs, such as foregone profits and costs passed onto consumers, as well as direct costs and, when requested by the chair or ranking Member of a committee, the prospective costs of legislation that would change conditions of federal financial assistance. These two bills, as well as H.R. 5818, the Mandate Prevention Act of 2010, would also make private-sector mandates subject to a substantive point of order. H.R. 373, H.R. 4078, S. 1189, the Unfunded Mandates Accountability Act of 2011, its companion bill in the House, H.R. 2964, and S. 1720, the Jobs Through Growth Act: Title VII, the Unfunded Mandates Accountability Act, would also remove UMRA's exemption for rules issued by most independent agencies. Other organizations have argued that UMRA's coverage should be maintained or reinforced by adding exclusions for mandates regarding public health, safety, workers' rights, environmental protection, and the disabled.

This report examines debates over what constitutes an unfunded federal mandate and UMRA's implementation. It focuses on UMRA's requirement that CBO issue written cost estimate statements for federal mandates in legislation, its procedures for raising points of order in the House and Senate concerning unfunded federal mandates in legislation, and its requirement that federal agencies prepare written cost estimate statements for federal mandates in rules. It also assesses UMRA's impact on federal mandates and arguments concerning UMRA's future, focusing on UMRA's definitions, exclusions, and exceptions which currently exempt many federal actions with potentially significant financial impacts on nonfederal entities. An examination of the rise of unfunded federal mandates as a national issue and a summary of UMRA's legislative history are provided in **Appendix A**. Citations to UMRA points of order raised in the House and Senate are provided in **Appendix B**.

Contents

Tables

Appendixes

Contacts

An Overview of UMRA, Its Origins, and Provisions

Overview

The Unfunded Mandates Reform Act of 1995 (UMRA) established requirements for enacting certain legislation and issuing certain regulations that would impose enforceable duties on state, local, or tribal governments or on the private sector.[1] UMRA refers to obligations imposed by such legislation and regulations as "mandates" (either "intergovernmental" or "private sector," depending on the entities affected). The direct cost to affected entities of meeting these obligations are referred to as "mandate costs," and when the federal government does not provide funding to cover these costs, the mandate is termed "unfunded."

UMRA incorporates numerous definitions, exclusions, and exceptions that specify what forms and types of mandates are subject to its requirements, termed "covered mandates." Covered mandates do not include many federal actions with potentially significant financial impacts on nonfederal entities. This report's primary purpose is to describe the kinds of legislative and regulatory provisions that are subject to UMRA's requirements, and, on this basis, to assess UMRA's impact on federal mandates. The report also examines debates that occurred, both before and since UMRA's enactment, concerning what kinds of provisions UMRA ought to cover, and considers the implications of experience under UMRA for possible future revisions of its scope of coverage.

This report also describes the requirements UMRA imposes on congressional and agency actions to establish covered mandates. For most legislation and regulations covered by UMRA, these requirements are only informational. For reported legislation that would impose covered mandates on the intergovernmental or private sectors, UMRA requires the Congressional Budget Office (CBO) to provide an estimate of mandate costs. Similarly, for regulations that would impose covered mandates on the intergovernmental or private sectors, UMRA requires that the issuing agency provide an estimate of mandate costs (although the specifics of the estimates required for legislation and for regulations differ somewhat). Also, solely for legislation that would impose covered intergovernmental mandates, UMRA establishes a point of order in each house of Congress through which the chamber can decline to consider the legislation. This report examines UMRA's implementation, focusing on the respective requirements for mandate cost estimates on legislation and regulations, and on the point of order procedure for legislation proposing unfunded intergovernmental mandates.

Origin

The concept of unfunded mandates rose to national prominence during the 1970s and 1980s primarily through the response of state and local government officials to changes in the nature of federal intergovernmental grant-in-aid programs and to regulations affecting state and local governments. Before then, the federal government had traditionally relied on the provision of voluntary grant-in-aid funding to encourage state and local governments to perform particular activities or provide particular services that were deemed to be in the national interest. These

---

[1] P.L. 104-4; 109 Stat. 48 *et seq.*; and 2 U.S.C. §602, 632, 653, 658-658(g), 1501-1504, 1511-1516, 1531-1538, 1551-1556, and 1571.

arrangements were viewed as reflecting, at least in part, the constitutional protections afforded state and local governments as separate, sovereign entities. During the 1970s and 1980s, however, state and local government advocates argued that a "dramatic shift" occurred in the way the federal government dealt with states and localities. Instead of relying on the technique of subsidization to achieve its goals, the federal government was increasingly relying on "new, more intrusive, and more compulsory" programs and regulations that required compliance under the threat of civil or criminal penalties, imposed federal fiscal sanctions for failure to comply with the programs' requirements, or preempted state and local government authority to act in the area.[2] These new, more intrusive, and compulsory programs and regulations came to be referred to as "unfunded mandates" on states and localities.

State and local government advocates viewed these unfunded federal intergovernmental mandates as inconsistent with the traditional view of American federalism, which was based on cooperation, not compulsion. They argued that a federal statute was needed to forestall federal legislation and regulations that imposed obligations on state and local governments that resulted in higher costs and inefficiencies. UMRA's enactment in 1995 culminated years of effort by state and local government officials to control, if not eliminate, the imposition of unfunded federal mandates.

Advocates of regulatory reform adapted the concept of unfunded mandates to their view that federal regulations often impose financial burdens on private enterprise. Critics of government regulation of business argued that these regulations impose unfunded mandates on the private sector, just as federal programs and regulations impose fiscal obligations on state and local governments. As a result, various business organizations subject to increased federal regulation came to support state and local government efforts to enact federal legislation to control unfunded federal intergovernmental mandates. Private-sector advocates argued that they, too, should be provided relief from what they viewed as burdensome federal regulations that hinder economic growth.[3] Subsequently, proposals to control unfunded mandates that were developed in the early 1990s contained provisions addressing not only federal intergovernmental mandates, but federal private-sector mandates as well.

During floor debate on legislation that became UMRA, sponsors of the measure emphasized its role in bringing "our system of federalism back into balance, by serving as a check against the easy imposition of unfunded mandates."[4] Opponents argued that federal mandates may be necessary to achieve national objectives in areas where voluntary action by state and local governments or business failed to achieve desired results. See the **Appendix A** for a more detailed examination of the rise of unfunded federal mandates as a national issue and of UMRA's legislative history.[5]

---

[2] U.S. Advisory Commission on Intergovernmental Relations (ACIR), *Regulatory Federalism: Policy, Process, Impact, and Reform*, A-95 (Washington, DC: ACIR, 1984), pp. 1-18.

[3] Mary McElvenn, "The Federal Impact on Business," *Nation's Business*, vol. 79, no. 1 (January 1991), pp. 23-26; David Warner, "Regulations' Staggering Costs," *Nation's Business*, vol. 80, no. 6 (June 1992), pp. 50-53; Michael Barrier, "Taxing the Man Behind the Tree," *Nation's Business*, vol. 81, no. 9 (September 1993), pp. 31, 32; and Michael Barrier, "Mandates Foes Smell a Victory," *Nation's Business*, vol. 82, no. 9 (September 1994), p. 50.

[4] Senator Dirk Kempthorne, "Unfunded Mandate Reform Act," remarks in the Senate, *Congressional Record*, vol. 141, part 1 (January 12, 1995), p. 1166.

[5] Senator Frank Lautenberg, "Unfunded Mandate Reform Act," remarks in the Senate, *Congressional Record*, vol. 141, part 1 (January 12, 1995), p. 1193.

Summary of UMRA's Provisions

The congressional commitment to reshaping intergovernmental relations through UMRA is reflected in its eight statutory purposes:

(1) to strengthen the partnership between the Federal Government and State, local, and tribal governments;

(2) to end the imposition, in the absence of full consideration by Congress, of Federal mandates on State, local, and tribal governments without adequate Federal funding, in a manner that may displace other essential State, local, and tribal governmental priorities;

(3) to assist Congress in its consideration of proposed legislation establishing or revising Federal programs containing Federal mandates affecting State, local, and tribal governments, and the private sector by—(A) providing for the development of information about the nature and size of mandates in proposed legislation; and (B) establishing a mechanism to bring such information to the attention of the Senate and the House of Representatives before the Senate and the House of Representatives vote on proposed legislation;

(4) to promote informed and deliberate decisions by Congress on the appropriateness of Federal mandates in any particular instance;

(5) to require that Congress consider whether to provide funding to assist State, local, and tribal governments in complying with Federal mandates, to require analyses of the impact of private sector mandates, and through the dissemination of that information provide informed and deliberate decisions by Congress and Federal agencies and retain competitive balance between the public and private sectors;

(6) to establish a point-of-order vote on the consideration in the Senate and House of Representatives of legislation containing significant Federal intergovernmental mandates without providing adequate funding to comply with such mandates;

(7) to assist Federal agencies in their consideration of proposed regulations affecting State, local, and tribal governments, by—(A) requiring that Federal agencies develop a process to enable the elected and other officials of State, local, and tribal governments to provide input when Federal agencies are developing regulations; and (B) requiring that Federal agencies prepare and consider estimates of the budgetary impact of regulations containing Federal mandates upon State, local, and tribal governments and the private sector before adopting such regulations, and ensuring that small governments are given special consideration in that process; and

(8) to begin consideration of the effect of previously imposed Federal mandates, including the impact on State, local, and tribal governments of Federal court interpretations of Federal statutes and regulations that impose Federal intergovernmental mandates.[6]

To achieve its purposes, UMRA's Title I established a procedural framework to shape congressional deliberations concerning covered unfunded intergovernmental and private-sector mandates. This framework requires CBO to estimate the direct mandate costs of intergovernmental mandates exceeding $50 million and of private-sector mandates exceeding $100 million (in any fiscal year) proposed in any measure reported from committee. It also

---

[6] 2 U.S.C. §1501.

establishes a point of order against consideration of legislation that contained intergovernmental mandates with mandate costs estimated to exceed the threshold amount. In addition, Title II requires federal administrative agencies, unless otherwise prohibited by law, to assess the effects on state and local governments and the private sector of proposed and final federal rules and to prepare a written statement of estimated costs and benefits for any mandate requiring an expenditure exceeding $100 million in any given year. All threshold amounts under these provisions are adjusted annually for inflation.[7]

In general, the requirements of Titles I and II apply to any provision in legislation, statute, or regulation that would impose an enforceable duty upon state and local governments or the private sector. However, UMRA does not apply to conditions of federal assistance, duties stemming from participation in voluntary federal programs, rules issued by independent regulatory agencies, or rules issued without a general notice of proposed rulemaking. Exceptions also exist for rules and legislative provisions that cover individual constitutional rights, discrimination, emergency assistance, grant accounting and auditing procedures, national security, treaty obligations, and certain elements of Social Security legislation.[8]

UMRA's Title III also called for a review of federal intergovernmental mandates to be completed by the now-defunct U.S. Advisory Commission on Intergovernmental Relations (ACIR) within 18 months of enactment.[9] ACIR completed a preliminary report on federal intergovernmental mandates in January 1996, but the final report was not released.[10] Finally, UMRA's Title IV authorizes judicial review of federal agency compliance with Title II provisions.[11]

What Is an Unfunded Federal Mandate?

One of the first issues Congress faced when considering unfunded federal mandate legislation was how to define the concept. For example, during a November 3, 1993, congressional hearing on unfunded mandate legislation, Senator Judd Gregg argued,

> Any bill reported out this committee [Governmental Affairs] should precisely define what constitutes an unfunded federal mandate.... An appropriate definition is crucial because it will drive almost everything else that occurs. Without a precise definition, endless litigation would likely ensue over what is and what is not an unfunded federal mandate. A true solution to the problem cannot allow it to become more cost-effective to pay the bills than to seek payment. Furthermore, the definition cannot be too restrictive. It would solve nothing to

---

[7] 2 U.S.C §658; and 2 U.S.C. §1532.

[8] 2 U.S.C 658(5)(A), (7)(A) and (10), and 2 U.S.C. §1503.

[9] 2 U.S.C. §1551-1553.

[10] ACIR funding was withdrawn following the release for public comment and a hearing on the draft report on federal mandates. ACIR was required by UMRA to conduct the study and to make recommendations for mitigating the effect mandates have on state and local governments. The draft report recommended the elimination of a number of federal mandates which had strong support in Congress. ACIR's commission members decided not to release the report in a party-line vote. Most observers concluded that the draft report was a contributing factor in ACIR's losing its funding. See, John Kincaid, "Review of 'The Politics of Unfunded Mandates: Whither Federalism?' by Paul L. Posner," *Political Science Quarterly*, vol. 114, no. 2 (Summer 1999), pp. 322-323.

[11] 2 U.S.C. §1571.

cut off one particular type of unfunded mandate, only to prompt Congressional use of another to accelerate.[12]

The difficulty Congress faced in defining the concept was that there were strong disagreements, among academics, practitioners, and elected officials, over how to define it. These disagreements appear motivated by concerns about which classes of costs incurred by state and local governments (or the private sector) should be identified and controlled for in the legislative or regulatory process. They have typically been conducted, however, as disputes about which classes of such costs are properly considered as obligatory requirements on the affected entities. The resulting focus on whether or not particular kinds of costs are "mandatory" has tended to obscure consideration of the core policy question concerning what kinds of costs should be subjected to informational requirements or procedural restrictions such as those that UMRA establishes.

Competing Definitions

In 1979, one set of federalism scholars defined unfunded federal intergovernmental mandates broadly as including "any responsibility, action, procedure, or anything else that is imposed by constitutional, administrative, executive, or judicial action as a direct order or that is required as a condition of aid."[13] In 1984, ACIR offered a rationale for defining unfunded federal intergovernmental mandates which excluded conditions of aid. ACIR argued that defining unfunded federal intergovernmental mandates was difficult because federal grant-in-aid programs typically include both incentives and mandates backed by sanctions or penalties:

> Few federal programs affecting state and local governments are pure types.... Every grant-in-aid program, including General Revenue Sharing, the least restrictive form of aid, comes with federal "strings" attached. Here, as in other areas, there is no such thing as a free lunch....
>
> In the intergovernmental sphere, then, [mandates] and subsidy are less like different parts of a dichotomy than opposing ends of a continuum. At one extreme is the general support grant with just a few associated conditions or rules; at the other is the costly, but wholly unfunded, national "mandate." In between are many programs combining subsidy and [mandate] approaches, in varying degrees and in various ways.[14]

ACIR argued that because federal grant-in-aid programs typically combine subsidy and mandate approaches, grant-in-aid programs should be classified according to their degree of compulsion. It argued that conditions of grant aid should not be classified as a mandate because "one of the most important features of the grant-in-aid is that its acceptance is still viewed legally as entirely voluntary" and "although it is difficult for many jurisdictions to forego substantial financial benefits, this option remains real."[15] ACIR also argued that most grant conditions affect only the

---

[12] U.S. Congress, Senate Committee on Governmental Affairs, *Federal Mandates on State and Local Governments,* 103rd Cong., 1st sess., November 3, 1993, S.Hrg. 103-405 (Washington: GPO, 1994), p. 66.

[13] Catherine H. Lovell, Max Neiman, Robert Kneisel, Adam Rose, and Charles Tobin, *Federal and State Mandating on Local Governments: Report to the National Science Foundation* (Riverside, CA: University of California, June 1979), p. 32.

[14] ACIR, *Regulatory Federalism: Policy, Process, Impact, and Reform,* A-95 (Washington, DC: ACIR, 1984), p. 4.

[15] Ibid. The Supreme Court has emphasized the voluntary nature of federal grant programs and the fact that states and private parties remain free to accept or reject the offer of federal funds and thus avoid the attached conditions. "This Court has repeatedly upheld against constitutional challenge the use of this technique to induce governments and private parties to cooperate voluntarily with federal policy." Fullilove v. Klutznick, 448 U.S. 448, 474 (1980) (Chief (continued...)

administration of those activities funded by the program, and "grants-in-aid generally provide significant benefits to the recipient jurisdiction."[16]

ACIR argued that federal grant-in-aid programs that "cannot be side-stepped, without incurring some federal sanction, by the simple expedient of refusing to participate in a single federal assistance program" should be considered mandates.[17] ACIR provided four examples of federal activities that, in the absence of sufficient compensatory funding, could be an unfunded intergovernmental mandate: (1) direct legal orders that must be complied with under the threat of civil or criminal penalties; (2) crosscutting or generally applicable requirements imposed on grants across the board to further national social and economic policies; (3) programs that impose federal fiscal sanctions in one program area or activity to influence state and local government policy in another area; and (4) federal preemption of state and local government law.[18]

In 1994, several organizations representing state and local governments issued a set of unfunded mandate principles which defined unfunded federal intergovernmental mandates as

- any federal requirement that compels state or local activities resulting in additional state or local expenditures;

- any federal requirement that imposes additional conditions or increases the level of state and local expenditures needed to maintain eligibility for existing federal grants;

- any reduction in the rate of federal matching for existing grants; and

- any federal requirement that reduces the productivity of existing state or local taxes and fees and/or that increases the cost of raising state and local revenue (including the costs of borrowing).[19]

Also in 1994, ACIR introduced the term "federally induced costs" to replace what it described as "the pejorative and definitional baggage associated with the term 'mandates.'"[20] ACIR identified the following types of federal activities that expose states and localities to additional costs:

- statutory direct orders;

- total and partial statutory preemptions;

- grant-in-aid conditions on spending and administration, including matching requirements;

- federal income tax provisions;

(...continued)

Justice Burger announcing judgment of the Court); see also *South Dakota v. Dole*, 483 U.S. 203 (1987).

[16] Ibid.

[17] Ibid., p. 7.

[18] Ibid., pp. 7-10.

[19] National Conference of State Legislatures, "Unfunded Mandate Principles," Washington, DC, 1994, p. 1 cited in CRS Report 95-62, *Mandates and the Congress*, by Sandra S. Osbourn (out of print, available by request).

[20] ACIR, *Federally Induced Costs Affecting State and Local Governments*, M-193 (Washington, DC: ACIR, 1994), p. 3.

- federal court decisions; and

- administrative rules issued by federal agencies, including regulatory delays and non-enforcement.[21]

ACIR defended its inclusion of grant-in-aid conditions in its list of "federally induced costs," which it had excluded from its definition of federal mandates a decade earlier, by asserting that although the option of refusing to accept federal grants "seemed plausible when federal aid constituted a small and highly compartmentalized part of state and local revenues, it overlooks current realities. Many grant conditions have become far more integral to state and local activities—and far less subject to voluntary forbearance—than originally suggested by the contractual model."[22]

On April 28, 1994, John Kincaid, ACIR's executive director, testified at a congressional hearing that legislation concerning unfunded mandates "should recognize that unfunded Federal mandates include, in reality, a range of Federally-induced costs for which reimbursements may be legitimate considerations."[23] State and local government officials generally advocated the inclusion of ACIR's "federally induced costs" in legislation placing conditions on the imposition of unfunded intergovernmental mandates. However, organizations representing various environmental and social groups, such as the Committee on the Appointment of People With Disabilities, the Natural Resources Defense Council, the American Federation of State, County, and Municipal Employees, and the Service Employees International Union, argued that ACIR's definition was too broad. These groups testified at various congressional hearings that some federal mandates, particularly those involving the environment and constitutional rights, should be retained, even if they were unfunded.[24]

Statutory Direct Orders

With respect to definitions, there was, and continues to be, a general consensus among federalism scholars, state and local government officials, and other organizations that federal policies which impose unavoidable costs on state and local governments or business are, in the absence of sufficient compensatory funding, unfunded federal mandates. Because statutory direct orders, such as the Equal Employment Opportunity Act of 1972, which bars employment discrimination on the basis of race, color, religion, sex, and national origin, are compulsory, they are considered federal mandates. In the absence of sufficient compensatory funding, they are unfunded federal mandates. However, there was, and continues to be, a general consensus that some statutory direct orders, particularly those involving the guarantee of constitutional rights, should be exempt from legislation placing conditions on the imposition of unfunded federal mandates.[25] For

---

[21] Ibid., p. 19. ACIR also included laws that expose state and local governments to liability lawsuits, which, at the time, affected such programs as the Superfund toxic wastes cleanup program.

[22] Ibid., p. 20.

[23] U.S. Congress, Senate Committee on Governmental Affairs, *Federal Mandate Reform Legislation*, 103rd Cong., 2nd sess., April 28, 1994, S.Hrg. 103-1019 (Washington: GPO, 1995), p. 56.

[24] Ibid., pp. 53-55, 57-63, 68-70, 162-185, 200-230 and 247-249; U.S. Congress, Senate Committee on Governmental Affairs and Senate Committee on the Budget; U.S. Congress, Senate Committee on Governmental Affairs, *Federal Mandates on State and Local Governments*, 103rd Cong., 1st sess., November 3, 1993, S.Hrg. 103-405 (Washington: GPO, 1994), p. 241-245; and U.S. Congress, Senate Committee on Governmental Affairs, *S. 1 - Unfunded Mandates*, 104th Cong., 1st sess., January 5, 1995, S.Hrg. 104-392 (Washington: GPO, 1995), pp. 90-107.

[25] U.S. Government Accountability Office, *Unfunded Mandates: Views Vary About Reform Act's Strengths*, (continued...)

---

example, on April 28, 1994, Governor (now Senator) Benjamin Nelson, testifying on behalf of the National Governors Association at a congressional hearing on unfunded mandate legislation, argued,

> At the outset, Mr. Chairman, I want to make it absolutely crystal clear that the Governors' position opposing unfunded environmental mandates must not be interpreted as an effort to discontinue environmental legislation and regulations or oppose any individual's civil or constitutional rights. The Governors consider the protection of public health and State natural resources as among the most important responsibilities of our office. We all take an oath of office to protect the health and safety of our citizens. In addition, we have worked with Congress over the years to enact strong Federal environmental laws.[26]

Total and Partial Statutory Preemptions

Total and partial preemptions of state and local spending and regulatory authority by the federal government are compulsory, but there was, and continues to be, disagreement concerning whether they should be considered federal mandates, or whether they should be included in legislation designed to provide relief from unfunded federal mandates. Total preemptions in the intergovernmental arena prevent state and local government officials from implementing their own programs in a policy area. For example, states have been "stripped of their powers to engage in economic regulation of airlines, bus, and trucking companies, to establish a compulsory retirement age for their employees other than specified state policymakers and judges, or to regulate bankruptcies with the exception of the establishment of a homestead exemption."[27]

Partial preemption typically is a joint enterprise, "whereby the federal government exerts its constitutional authority to preempt a field and establish minimum national standards, but allows regulatory administration to be delegated to the states if they adopt standards at least as strict as the federal rules."[28] Legally, the state decision to administer a partial preemption program is voluntary. States that do not have a program in a particular area or do not wish to assume the costs of administration and enforcement can opt out and allow the federal government to enforce the standards.[29] Nonetheless, the federal standards apply.

Total and partial statutory preemptions are distinct from unfunded federal intergovernmental mandates because they do not necessarily impose costs or require state and local governments to take action. Nonetheless, some federalism scholars and state and local government officials have argued that total and partial statutory preemptions should be included in legislation placing conditions on the imposition of unfunded federal mandates because they can have similar adverse

---

(...continued)

Weaknesses, and Options for Improvement, GAO-05-454, March 31, 2005, pp. 9, 13, 14, at http://www.gao.gov/new.items/d05454.pdf.

[26] U.S. Congress, Senate Committee on Governmental Affairs, *Federal Mandate Reform Legislation*, 103rd Cong., 2nd sess., April 28, 1994, S.Hrg. 103-1019 (Washington: GPO, 1995), p. 7.

[27] Joseph F. Zimmerman, "National-State Relations: Cooperative Federalism in the Twentieth Century," *Publius: The Journal of Federalism*, vol. 31, no. 2 (Spring 2001), p. 23.

[28] ACIR, *Federally Induced Costs Affecting State and Local Governments*, M-193 (Washington, DC: ACIR, 1994), p. 22.

[29] Ibid., p. 23.

---

effects on state and local government flexibilities and, in some instances, resources.[30] A leading federalism scholar identified 557 federal preemption statutes as of 2005.[31]

Others argue that because total and partial preemptions are distinct from unfunded federal mandates, they should not be included in legislation placing conditions on the imposition of unfunded federal mandates. In addition, some business organizations oppose including preemptions in any law or definition involving unfunded federal mandates because federal preemptions can result in the standardization of regulation across state and local jurisdictions, an outcome favored by some business interests, particularly those with interstate and global operations.[32]

Grant-in-Aid Conditions

Conditions of grants-in-aid are generally not considered unfunded mandates because the costs they impose on state and local governments can be avoided by refusing the grant. However, federalism scholars and state and local government officials have argued that, in the absence of sufficient compensatory funding, grant conditions should be considered unfunded federal intergovernmental mandates, even though the grants themselves are voluntary.[33] In their view, federal "grants often require major commitments of state resources, changes in state laws, and even constitutional provisions to conform to a host of federal policy and administrative requirements" and that some grant programs, such as Medicaid, are "too large for state and local governments to voluntarily turn down, or when new and onerous conditions are added some time after state and local governments have become dependent on the program."[34] For example, on April 28, 1994, Patrick Sweeney, a Democratic member of Ohio's state House of Representatives testifying on behalf of the National Conference of State Legislatures (NCSL), asserted at a congressional hearing on unfunded mandate legislation that

> A great majority of the current problem can be attributed to Federal entitlements that are defined but then not adequately funded, and the proliferation of a mandatory requirement for what previously were voluntary programs. Programs like Medicaid are voluntary in theory only. A State cannot unilaterally opt out of Medicaid at any time it wishes, once it is in the program, without having to obtain a Federal waiver or face certain lawsuits.[35]

---

[30] U.S. Government Accountability Office, *Unfunded Mandates: Views Vary About Reform Act's Strengths, Weaknesses, and Options for Improvement*, GAO-05-454, March 31, 2005, pp. 5, 11, 12, 23, 38, 39, 43, 47, 48, at http://www.gao.gov/new.items/d05454.pdf.

[31] Joseph F. Zimmerman, "Congressional Preemption During the George W. Bush Administration," *Publius: The Journal of Federalism*, vol. 37, no. 3 (Summer 2007), p. 436.

[32] U.S. Government Accountability Office, *Unfunded Mandates: Views Vary About Reform Act's Strengths, Weaknesses, and Options for Improvement*, GAO-05-454, March 31, 2005, p. 12, at http://www.gao.gov/new.items/d05454.pdf; and Paul L. Posner, "The Politics of Preemption: Prospects for the States," *PS* (July 2005), p. 372.

[33] Paul L. Posner, "Mandates: The Politics of Coercive Federalism," in *Intergovernmental Management for the 21st Century*, eds. Timothy J. Conlan and Paul L. Posner (Washington, DC: Brookings Institution Press, 2008), p. 287; and Paul L. Posner, *The Politics of Unfunded Mandates: Whither Federalism?* (Washington, DC: Georgetown University Press, 1998), pp. 4, 12-14.

[34] Paul L. Posner, *The Politics of Unfunded Mandates: Whither Federalism?* (Washington, DC: Georgetown University Press, 1998), pp. 12, 13. See also, Joseph F. Zimmerman, "Federally Induced State and Local Government Costs," paper delivered at the 1991 Annual Meeting of the American Political Science Association, Washington, DC, September 1, 1991, p. 4.

[35] U.S. Congress, Senate Committee on Governmental Affairs, *Federal Mandate Reform Legislation*, 103rd Cong., 2nd sess., April 28, 1994, S.Hrg. 103-1019 (Washington: GPO, 1995), p. 11.

Federal Tax Provisions

Federalism scholars, state and local government officials, and other organizations argue that federal tax policies that preempt state and local authority to tax specific activities or entities are unfunded mandates, and should be covered under legislation placing restrictions on unfunded mandates, because the fiscal impact of preempting state or local government revenue sources cannot be avoided and "can be every bit as costly" as mandates ordering state or local government action.[36] For example, the Internet Tax Freedom Act Amendments Act of 2007 extended the moratorium on internet taxation through November 1, 2014.[37] The NCSL has estimated that states could receive an additional $23.3 billion annually in state sales tax revenue if the moratorium were lifted.[38]

In addition, because most state and local income taxes have been designed purposively to conform with federal tax law, changes in federal tax policy can impact state and local government finances. For example, federal tax cuts adopted in 2001 and 2003 affecting depreciation, dividends, and estate taxes "forced states to acquiesce and accept their consequences or decouple from the federal tax base."[39] Yet, federal tax changes are generally considered not to be unfunded mandates because states and localities can avoid their costs by decoupling their income tax from the federal income tax. Nevertheless, because federal tax changes can affect state and local government tax bases, most state and local government officials advocate their inclusion in federal legislation placing conditions on the imposition of unfunded federal mandates.

Federal Court Decisions; Administrative Rules Issued by Federal Agencies; and Regulatory Delays and Non-enforcement

Federalism scholars, state and local government officials, and other organizations argue that, in the absence of sufficient compensatory funding, court decisions and regulatory actions taken by federal agencies, including regulatory delays and non-enforcement, are unfunded mandates and should be included in legislation placing conditions on the imposition of unfunded mandates because these actions can impose costs on state and local governments that cannot be avoided. UMRA's provisions concerning administrative rules are discussed in greater detail later in this report (see the section on "UMRA and Federal Rulemaking (Title II)."

UMRA's Definition of an Unfunded Federal Mandate

After taking various definitions into consideration, Congress defined federal mandates in UMRA more narrowly than state and local government officials had hoped. Federal intergovernmental mandates were defined as any provision in legislation, statute, or regulation that "would impose

---

[36] National Conference of State Legislatures, "Policy Position on Federal Mandate Relief," effective through August 2011, at http://www.ncsl.org/Default.aspx?TabID=773&tabs=855,20,632#FederalMandate; and Paul L. Posner, "Mandates: The Politics of Coercive Federalism," in *Intergovernmental Management for the 21ˢᵗ Century*, eds. Timothy J. Conlan and Paul L. Posner (Washington, DC: Brookings Institution Press, 2008), pp. 287, 292, 293.

[37] For further analysis, see CRS Report RL33261, *Internet Taxation: Issues and Legislation*, by Steven Maguire and Nonna A. Noto.

[38] National Conference of State Legislatures, "Collecting E-Commerce Taxes," Washington, DC.

[39] Paul L. Posner, "Mandates: The Politics of Coercive Federalism," in *Intergovernmental Management for the 21ˢᵗ Century*, eds. Timothy J. Conlan and Paul L. Posner (Washington, DC: Brookings Institution Press, 2008), p. 292.

---

an enforceable duty upon State, local, or tribal governments" or "reduce or eliminate the amount" of federal funding authorized to cover the costs of an existing mandate.[40] Provisions in legislation, statute, or regulation that "would increase the stringency of conditions of assistance" or "would place caps upon, or otherwise decrease" federal funding for existing intergovernmental grants with annual entitlement authority of $500 million or more could also be considered a federal intergovernmental mandate, but only if the state, local, or tribal government "lack authority under that program to amend their financial or programmatic responsibilities to continue providing required services that are affected by the legislation, statute, or regulation."[41]

Private-sector mandates were defined as "any provision in legislation, statute, or regulation that would impose an enforceable duty upon the private sector" or "reduce or eliminate the amount" of federal funding authorized "for the purposes of ensuring compliance with such duty."[42]

Key words in both definitions are "enforceable duty." Because statutory direct orders, total and partial preemptions, federal tax policies that preempt specific state and local tax policies, and administrative rules issued by federal agencies cannot be avoided, they are enforceable duties and are covered under UMRA. In contrast, because federal grants are voluntary, grant conditions are not considered enforceable duties and, therefore, are not covered under UMRA. Federal tax policies that impose costs on state and local governments that can be avoided by decoupling the state or local government's affected income tax provision from the federal income tax code are not enforceable duties, and, therefore, also are not covered under UMRA.

UMRA considers a mandate unfunded unless the legislation authorizing the mandate fully meets its estimated direct costs by either (1) providing new budget authority (direct spending authority or entitlement authority) or (2) authorizing appropriations. If appropriations are authorized, the mandate is still considered unfunded unless the legislation ensures that in any fiscal year, either (1) the actual costs of the mandate are estimated not to exceed the appropriations actually provided; (2) the terms of the mandate will be revised so that it can be carried out with the funds appropriated; (3) the mandate will be abolished; or (4) Congress will enact new legislation to continue the mandate as an unfunded mandate.[43] This mechanism for reviewing and revising mandates on the basis of their actual costs, which was introduced into UMRA in the "Byrd lookback amendment" (as described in the **Appendix A**), applies only to intergovernmental mandates enacted in legislation as funded through appropriations.

Exemptions and Exclusions

UMRA generally excluded pre-existing federal mandates from its provisions, but, as mentioned previously, it did include any provision in legislation, statute, or regulation that "would increase the stringency of conditions of assistance" or "would place caps upon, or otherwise decrease" federal funding for existing intergovernmental grants with annual entitlement authority of $500 million or more.[44] However, this provision applies "only if the state or locality lacks authority to amend its financial or programmatic responsibilities to continue providing the required

---

[40] 2 U.S.C. §658(5)(A).

[41] 2 U.S.C. §658(5)(B).

[42] 2 U.S.C. §658(7)(A) and 2 U.S.C. §658(7)(B).

[43] 2 U.S.C. §658d(a)(2); §425 of the Congressional Budget and Impoundment Control Act of 1974, as amended, P.L. 93-344, 88 Stat. 297, 2 U.S.C. §658 *et seq.*

[44] 2 U.S.C. §658(5)(B).

services."[45] Because CBO has determined that many large intergovernmental entitlement grant programs, such as Medicaid and Temporary Assistance to Needy Families, "allow states significant flexibility to alter their programs and accommodate new requirements," UMRA provisions have not been applied to them.[46]

UMRA's Title I does not apply to conditions of federal assistance; duties stemming from participation in voluntary federal programs; and legislative provisions that cover individual constitutional rights, discrimination, emergency assistance, grant accounting and auditing procedures, national security, treaty obligations, and certain parts of Social Security relating to the old-age, survivors, and disability insurance program under title II of the Social Security Act.[47]

UMRA did not indicate that these exempted provisions and rules were not federal mandates. Instead, it established that their costs would not be subject to its provisions requiring written cost estimate statements, or to its provisions permitting a point of order to be raised against the consideration of reported legislation in which they appear. The Senate Committee on Governmental Affairs report accompanying S. 1, The Unfunded Mandate Reform Act of 1995, provided its reasoning for adopting the exempted provisions and rules:

> A number of these exemptions are standard in many pieces of legislation in order to recognize the domain of the President in foreign affairs and as Commander-in-Chief as well as to ensure that Congress's and the Executive Branch's hands are not tied with procedural requirements in times of national emergencies. Further, the Committee thinks that Federal auditing, accounting and other similar requirements designed to protect Federal funds from potential waste, fraud, and abuse should be exempt from the Act.
>
> The Committee recognizes the special circumstances and history surrounding the enactment and enforcement of Federal civil rights laws. During the middle part of the 20th century, the arguments of those who opposed the national, uniform extension of basic equal rights, protection, and opportunity to all individuals were based on a States rights philosophy. With the passage of the Civil Rights Acts of 1957 and 1964 and the Voting Rights Act of 1965, Congress rejected that argument out of hand as designed to thwart equal opportunity and to protect discriminatory, unjust and unfair practices in the treatment of individuals in certain parts of the country. The Committee therefore exempts Federal civil rights laws from the requirements of this Act.[48]

In addition, as will be discussed in the next section, UMRA does not require all legislative provisions that contain federal mandates, even those that contain mandates that meet UMRA's definition, to have a CBO written cost estimate statement. In some instances, CBO may determine that cost estimates may not be feasible or complete. In addition, UMRA only requires estimates of direct costs imposed by the legislation. Estimates of indirect, secondary costs, such

---

[45] U.S. Congress, Senate Committee on Finance, *Work, Opportunity, and Responsibility for Kids Act*, report to accompany H.R. 4737, 107th Cong., 2nd sess., July 25, 2002, S.Rept. 107-221 (Washington: GPO, 2002), p. 61; and 2 U.S.C. §658(5)(B).

[46] U.S. Congress, Senate Committee on Finance, *Work, Opportunity, and Responsibility for Kids Act*, report to accompany H.R. 4737, 107th Cong., 2nd sess., July 25, 2002, S.Rept. 107-221 (Washington: GPO, 2002), p. 61.

[47] 2 U.S.C. §658a.

[48] U.S. Congress, Senate Committee on Governmental Affairs, *Unfunded Mandate Reform Act of 1995*, report to accompany S. 1, 104th Cong., 1st sess., January 11, 1995, S.Rept. 104-1 (Washington: GPO, 1995), p. 12.

as effects on prices and wages when the costs of a mandate imposed on one party are passed on to others, such as customers or employees, are not required.[49]

UMRA and Congressional Procedure (Title I)

UMRA's Procedures

Under Title I, which took effect on January 1, 1996, CBO was directed, to the extent practicable, to assist congressional committees, upon their request, in analyzing the budgetary and financial impact of any proposed legislation that may have (1) a significant budgetary impact on state, local, and tribal governments; (2) a significant financial impact on the private sector; or (3) a significant employment impact on the private sector. In addition, CBO was directed, if asked by a committee chair or committee ranking minority Member, to conduct a study, to the extent practicable, of the budgetary and financial impact of proposed legislation containing a federal mandate. If reasonably feasible, the study is to include estimates of the future direct costs of the federal mandate "to the extent that such costs significantly differ from or extend beyond the 5-year period after the mandate is first effective."[50]

While the actions noted above are technically discretionary, UMRA does contain mandatory directives. When an authorizing committee reports a public bill or joint resolution containing a federal mandate, UMRA requires the committee to provide the measure to CBO for budgetary analysis.[51] CBO is required to provide the committee a cost estimate statement of a mandate's direct costs if those costs are estimated to equal or exceed predetermined amounts, adjusted for inflation, in any of the first five fiscal years the legislation would be in effect. In 2012, those threshold amounts are $73 million for intergovernmental mandates and $146 million for private-sector mandates. CBO is also required to inform the committee if the mandate has estimated direct costs below these thresholds and briefly explain the basis of the estimate.

CBO must also identify any increase in federal appropriations or other spending that has been provided to fund the mandate.[52] The federal mandate is considered unfunded unless estimated costs are fully funded. As described above, under "UMRA's Definition of an Unfunded Federal Mandate," UMRA provides that mandate costs be considered as funded only if the legislation covers the mandate costs either by providing new direct spending or entitlement authority or by authorizing appropriations and incorporating a mechanism to provide for the mandate to be revised or abolished if the requisite appropriations are not provided.

Direct costs for intergovernmental mandates are defined as "the aggregate estimated amounts that all State, local and tribal governments would be required to spend or would be prohibited from raising in revenues in order to comply with the Federal intergovernmental mandate."[53] Direct costs for federal private-sector mandates are defined as "the aggregate estimated amounts that the

---

[49] U.S. General Accounting Office, *Unfunded Mandates: Analysis of Reform Act Coverage*, GAO-04-637, May 12, 2004, pp. 11-17, at http://www.gao.gov/new.items/d04637.pdf.

[50] 2 U.S.C. §602.

[51] 2 U.S.C. §658b.

[52] 2 U.S.C. §658c.

[53] 2 U.S.C. §658 (3)(A)(i).

private sector will be required to spend in order to comply with the Federal private sector mandate."[54]

To accomplish these tasks, CBO created the State and Local Government Cost Estimates Unit within its Budget Analysis Division to prepare intergovernmental mandate cost estimate statements as well as other analysis and special studies on the budgetary effects of mandates. It also added new staff to its program analysis divisions to prepare private-sector mandate cost estimate statements.[55]

A congressional committee is required to include the CBO estimate of mandate costs in its report on the bill. If the mandate cost estimate is not available, or if the report is not expected to be in print before the legislation reaches the floor for consideration, the committee is to publish the mandate cost estimate in the *Congressional Record* in advance of floor consideration. In addition to identifying direct costs, the committee's report must also assess the likely costs and benefits of any mandates in the legislation, describe how they affect the competitive balance between the private and public sectors, state the extent to which the legislation would preempt state, local or tribal law, and explain the effect of any preemption. For intergovernmental mandates alone, the committee is to describe in its report the extent to which the legislation authorizes federal funding for direct costs of the mandate, and detail whether and how funding is to be provided.[56]

CBO Cost Estimate Statements

As indicated in **Table 1**, CBO has submitted 9,397 estimates of mandate costs to Congress from January 1, 1996, when UMRA's Title I became effective, to October 18, 2012. Each of these statements examined the mandate costs imposed on the private sector or state, local, and tribal governments by provisions in a specific bill, amendment, or conference report. About 12.8% of these cost estimate statements (1,206 of 9,397 cost estimate statements) identified costs imposed by intergovernmental mandates on states and localities, and 1.0% of them (98 of 9,397 cost estimate statements) identified intergovernmental mandates that exceeded UMRA's threshold. CBO was unable to determine costs imposed by intergovernmental mandates in 76 bills, amendments, or conference reports.

**Table 1. CBO Estimates of Costs of Intergovernmental Mandates,
104th - 112th Congresses**

Congress	Cost Estimate Statements Transmitted	Statements With Identified Intergovernmental Mandates	Intergovernmental Mandate Costs Exceeding the Threshold	CBO Unable to Determine Mandate Costs
104th (1996)	718	69	11	6
105th (1997-1998)	1,062	128	14	14
106th (1999-2000)	1,279	158	7	1

---

[54] 2 U.S.C. §658 (3)(B).

[55] Theresa A. Gullo and Janet M. Kelly, "Federal Unfunded Mandate Reform: A First-Year Retrospective," *Public Administration Review*, vol. 58, no. 5 (September/October 1998), p. 381.

[56] 2 U.S.C. §658c(a).

Congress	Cost Estimate Statements Transmitted	Statements With Identified Intergovernmental Mandates	Intergovernmental Mandate Costs Exceeding the Threshold	CBO Unable to Determine Mandate Costs
107th (2001-2002)	1,038	110	10	8
108th (2003-2004)	1,172	152	16	7
109th (2005-2006)	978	171	18	6
110th (2007-2008)	1,382	168	7	6
111th (2009-2010)	893	134	11	19
112th (2011-October 18, 2012)	875	116	4	9
Total	9,397	1,206	98	76

Sources: U.S. Congressional Budget Office, "Cost Estimates," October 18, 2012, http://www.cbo.gov/search/ce_sitesearch.cfm; U.S. Congressional Budget Office, *A Review of CBO's Activities in 2011 Under the Unfunded Mandates Reform Act*, March 2012, p. 4; U.S. Congressional Budget Office, *A Review of CBO's Activities in 2010 Under the Unfunded Mandates Reform Act*, March 2011, p. 6; U.S. Congressional Budget Office, *A Review of CBO's Activities in 2008 Under the Unfunded Mandates Reform Act*, March 2009, p. 21; and U.S. Congressional Budget Office, *A Review of CBO's Activities Under the Unfunded Mandates Reform Act, 1996 to 2005*, March 2006, p. 4.

Notes: CBO began preparing mandate statements in January 1996. The figures for the 104th Congress reflect bills on the legislative calendar in January 1996 and bills reported by authorizing committees thereafter.

As indicated in **Table 2**, CBO has submitted 9,275 estimates to Congress that examined private-sector mandate costs imposed by provisions in a specific bill, amendment, or conference report from January 1, 1996, when UMRA's Title I became effective, to October 18, 2012. The number of statements transmitted to Congress shown in **Table 2** is less than the number shown in **Table 1** because CBO is sometimes asked to review a specific bill, amendment, or conference report solely for intergovernmental mandates.

About 16.2% of these private-sector estimates (1,500 of 9,275 cost estimate statements) identified costs imposed by mandates, and 4.0% of them (368 of 9,275 cost estimate statements) identified costs that exceeded UMRA's threshold. CBO was unable to determine costs imposed by private-sector mandates in 249 bills, amendments, or conference reports.

Table 2. CBO Estimate of Costs of Private-Sector Mandates, 104th - 112th Congresses

Congress	Cost Estimate Statements Transmitted	Statements With Identified Private-Sector Mandates	Private-Sector Mandate Costs Exceeding Threshold	CBO Unable to Determine Mandate Costs
104th (1996)	673	91	38	2
105th (1997-1998)	1,023	140	36	14
106th (1999-2000)	1,253	191	26	20
107th (2001-2002)	1,034	139	37	22
108th (2003-2004)	1,168	171	38	28
109th (2005-2006)	974	184	45	32
110th (2007-2008)	1,382	256	67	49

Congress	Cost Estimate Statements Transmitted	Statements With Identified Private-Sector Mandates	Private-Sector Mandate Costs Exceeding Threshold	CBO Unable to Determine Mandate Costs
111th (2009-2010)	893	190	41	50
112th (2011-October 18, 2012)	875	138	40	32
Total	9,275	1,500	368	249

Source: U.S. Congressional Budget Office, "Cost Estimates," October 18, 2012, http://www.cbo.gov/search/ce_sitesearch.cfm; U.S. Congressional Budget Office, *A Review of CBO's Activities in 2011 Under the Unfunded Mandates Reform Act*, March 2012, p. 4; U.S. Congressional Budget Office, *A Review of CBO's Activities in 2010 Under the Unfunded Mandates Reform Act*, March 2011, p. 6; U.S. Congressional Budget Office, *A Review of CBO's Activities in 2008 Under the Unfunded Mandates Reform Act*, March 2009, p. 21; and U.S. Congressional Budget Office, *A Review of CBO's Activities Under the Unfunded Mandates Reform Act, 1996 to 2005*, March 2006, p. 4.

Notes: CBO began preparing mandate statements in January 1996. The figures for the 104th Congress reflect bills on the legislative calendar in January 1996 and bills reported by authorizing committees thereafter. In some years, CBO transmitted more cost estimate statements for intergovernmental mandates than private-sector mandates because sometimes CBO was asked to review a specific bill, amendment, or conference report solely for intergovernmental mandates.

Points of Order for Initial Consideration

UMRA provides for the enforcement of its informational requirements on legislation by establishing a point of order in each chamber against consideration of a measure on which the reporting committee has not published the required estimate of mandate costs. This point of order applies only to measures reported by committees (for which CBO estimates of mandate costs are required), but it applies for both intergovernmental and private-sector mandates. In addition, however, if the informational requirement is met, a point of order against consideration of a measure may still be raised, if, for any fiscal year, the estimated total mandate cost of unfunded intergovernmental mandates in the measure exceeds UMRA's threshold amount ($73 million in 2012). This point of order may be raised also if CBO reported that no reasonable estimate of the cost of intergovernmental mandates was feasible.[57]

Uniquely among the requirements established by UMRA, this substantive point of order addressing intergovernmental mandates contained in legislation constitutes a potential means of control over the actual imposition of mandate costs. Even in this case, however, the mechanisms established by UMRA provide a means of controlling mandates only on the basis of estimates of the costs that will be incurred in subsequent fiscal years. The only provision of UMRA that offers a possibility of controls based on costs actually incurred by affected entities is the requirement, mentioned earlier, that a mandate can be considered funded through appropriations only if it directs that, if insufficient appropriations are made, the mandate must be revised, abolished, or reenacted as unfunded.

In several respects, the applicability of the substantive point of order differs from that of the informational point of order. First, it applies to any measure coming to the floor for consideration, whether or not reported by a committee, and also to conference reports. For a measure that has been reported, this point of order applies to the measure in the form reported, including, for

---

[57] 2 U.S.C. §658d(a); and 2 U.S.C. §658c(b)(3).

example, to a committee amendment in the nature of a substitute. In addition, this point of order applies against an amendment or motion (such as a motion to recommit with amendatory instructions), and does so on the basis not that the mandate costs of the amendment or motion itself exceeds the threshold, but that the amendment or motion would cause the total mandate costs in the measure to do so. Finally, however, this point of order applies only against intergovernmental mandates. UMRA imposes no comparable control in relation to private-sector mandates.

Because federal mandates are created through authorization bills, the UMRA points of order generally do not apply to bills reported by the House and Senate Committees on Appropriations. However, if an appropriation bill, resolution, amendment, or conference report contains legislative provisions that would either increase the direct costs of a federal intergovernmental mandate that exceeds the threshold, or cause those costs to exceed the threshold, a point of order may be raised against the provisions themselves. In the Senate, if this point of order is sustained, the provisions are stricken from the bill.[58]

In the House, the chair does not rule on a point of order raised under these provisions. Instead, the House, by majority vote, determines whether to consider the measure despite the point of order. To prevent dilatory use of the point of order, the chair need not put the question of consideration to a vote unless the Member making the point of order meets the "threshold burden" of identifying specific language that is claimed to contain the unfunded mandate. Also, if several points of order could be raised against the same measure, House practices under UMRA allow all of them to be disposed of at once by a single vote on consideration. If the Committee on Rules proposes a special rule for considering the measure that waives the point of order, UMRA subjects the special rule itself to a point of order, which is disposed of by the same mechanism.[59]

In the Senate, if questions are raised challenging the applicability of an UMRA point of order (e.g., to prevent its use for dilatory purposes), the presiding officer, to the extent practicable, consults with the Committee on Homeland Security and Governmental Affairs to determine if the measure contains an intergovernmental mandate and with the Senate Committee on the Budget to determine if the mandate's direct costs meet UMRA's threshold for allowing a point of order to be raised. The Senate Committee on the Budget may draw for this purpose on CBO cost estimate statements. If there are no such challenges, or the presiding officer rules against the challenge, the Senate determines whether to consider the measure despite the point of order. It may do so by voting on a motion to waive the point of order.[60]

Initially, a majority vote was necessary to waive the point of order in the Senate.[61] In 2005, the Senate increased its threshold to waive an UMRA point of order to 60 votes. Two UMRA points of order were raised in the Senate that year, and both were sustained, defeating two amendments to an appropriations bill that would have increased the minimum wage (see **Table 3**). In 2007, the Senate lowered its threshold to waive an UMRA point of order to a majority vote.[62]

---

[58] 2 U.S.C. §658d(c).

[59] 2 U.S.C. §658e(a); and 2 U.S.C. §658e(b)(3).

[60] 2 U.S.C. §658d(d); and 2 U.S.C. §658d(e).

[61] 2 U.S.C. §558d(a); §403(b)(1) of H.Con.Res. 95, adopted April 28, 2005.

[62] 2 U.S.C. §558d(a). A Senate amendment to S.Con.Res. 13, which was adopted on April 28, 2009, proposed to increase the vote necessary to waive the point of order in the Senate to 60. The amendment was initially agreed to by unanimous consent in the Senate, but was dropped in the final version.

A scholar familiar with UMRA has argued that, inasmuch as the general floor procedures of the Senate already allowed Senators to force a majority vote on a mandate by moving to strike it from the bill, UMRA's enforcement procedure of waiving a point of order by majority vote meant that UMRA mattered only in the House.[63] As evidence of this, the scholar noted that during UMRA's first 10 years of operation, when the threshold to waive an UMRA point of order was a majority vote in both the House and Senate, 13 UMRA points of order were raised, all in the House (see **Table 3**).

Table 3. UMRA Points of Order in the House and Senate, by Congress

Congress	Points of Order Raised in the House	Points of Order Sustained in the House	Points of Order Raised in the Senate	Points of Order Sustained in the Senate
104th (1996)	3	1	0	0
105th (1997-1998)	4	0	0	0
106th (1999-2000)	4	0	0	0
107th (2001-2002)	2	0	0	0
108th (2003-2004)	0	0	0	0
109th (2005-2006)	6	0	2	2
110th (2007-2008)	8	0	0	0
111th (2009-2010)	13	0	1	0
112th (2011-October 18, 2012)	10	0	0	0
Total	50	1	3	2

Source: *Congressional Record*, various years. A list of UMRA points of order raised to date is provided in **Appendix B**.

As indicated in **Table 3**, 50 UMRA points of order have been raised in the House. Only one of these points of order, the first one, which was raised on March 28, 1996, in opposition to a proposal to add a minimum wage increase to the Contract With America Advancement Act of 1996, resulted in the House voting to reject consideration of a proposed provision. During the 111th Congress and the 112th Congress, UMRA points of order in the House have often been raised not to challenge unfunded federal mandates *per se*, but to use the 10 minutes of debate allowed each House Member initiating an UMRA point of order to challenge the pace of legislative consideration, limitations on the offering of amendments to appropriations bills, or the inclusion of earmarks in legislation.[64]

Also, as indicated in **Table 3**, UMRA points of order have been raised in the Senate three times. In 2005, points of order were raised against two amendments relating to an increase in the minimum wage. In each case the Senate declined to waive the point of order, and the chair ruled that the amendment was out of order because it contained unfunded intergovernmental mandates in excess of the threshold.[65] In 2009, an UMRA point of order was raised against

---

[63] Elizabeth Garrett, "Framework Legislation and Federalism," *Notre Dame Law Review*, vol. 83, no. 4 (2008), p. 1502.

[64] Based on CRS review of the 23 points of order raised in the House, to date, during the 111th and 112th Congresses.

[65] "Transportation, Treasury, Housing and Urban Development, the Judiciary, the District of Columbia, and Independent Agencies Appropriations Act, 2006," proceedings in the Senate, *Congressional Record* (daily ed.) Vol. (continued...)

intergovernmental mandates in a health care reform bill.[66] The Senate voted to waive the point of order, 55-44.[67] The Senate subsequently approved the bill with the mandates.[68]

Impact on the Enactment of Statutory Intergovernmental and Private-Sector Mandates

Although UMRA points of order have been sustained just three times, most state and local government officials assert that UMRA has reduced "the number of unfunded federal mandates by acting as a deterrent to their enactment."[69] For example, NCSL's policy position on unfunded federal mandates asserts that

> Title I of UMRA—requiring the Congress to perform cost estimates and providing for a point of order—has been successful in reducing the number of unfunded mandates passed by the Congress. Further, the unfunded mandate point of order and other procedural mechanisms contained in UMRA have proven to be effective without impeding the legislative process.[70]

Also, Raymond Scheppach, NGA's executive director at that time, testified before a House subcommittee in 2001 that UMRA has slowed the growth of unfunded mandates and improved communications between federal policymakers and state and local government officials:

> Direct mandates have declined sharply in the wake of the Act. But I would venture that UMRA has had an even greater intangible benefit. As Congressman Portman once told us, he was certain this would be one of those bills that he could frame and hang on his wall, and it would become just another relic of history. But, to his surprise, the Act has led – time and again—to members asking his advice: "Do you think this bill will cause an UMRA problem? With whom should I work?" The very threat of a CBO report has engendered efforts to reach out to state and local leaders before the fact—instead of after. It has changed the nature of our intergovernmental discussion in a very positive way.[71]

In addition, there have been documented instances in which either sponsors of legislation have modified provisions to avoid a CBO statement that unfunded intergovernmental mandate costs

(...continued)

151, October 19, 2005, pp. S11526, S11547-S11548.

[66] Senator Robert Corker, "H.R. 3590, the Service Members Home Ownership Tax Act of 2009," remarks in the Senate, *Congressional Record*, daily edition, vol. 155, no. 199 (December 23, 2009), pp. S13803, S13804.

[67] "Consideration of H.R. 3590, the Service Members Home Ownership Tax Act of 2009, Senate Rollcall Vote No. 390," *Congressional Record*, daily edition, vol. 155, no. 199 (December 23, 2009), p. S13831.

[68] "Consideration of H.R. 3590, the Patient Protection and Affordable Care Act, Senate Rollcall Vote No. 396," *Congressional Record*, daily edition, vol. 155, no. 201 (December 24, 2009), p. S13831

[69] U.S. Government Accountability Office, *Unfunded Mandates: Views Vary About Reform Act's Strengths, Weaknesses, and Options for Improvement*, GAO-05-454, March 31, 2005, p. 15, at http://www.gao.gov/new.items/d05454.pdf.

[70] National Conference of State Legislatures, "Policy Position on Federal Mandate Relief," effective through August 2011, at http://www.ncsl.org/Default.aspx?TabID=773&tabs=855,20,632#FederalMandate.

[71] Joint Hearing, U.S. Congress, House Committee on Government Reform, Subcommittee on Energy Policy, Natural Resources and Regulatory Affairs, and House Committee on Rules, Subcommittee on Technology and the House, *Unfunded Mandates: A Five Year Review and Recommendations for Change*, hearing on the Unfunded Mandates Reform Act of 1995, 107th Cong., 1st sess., May 24, 2001, H. Hrg. 107-19 (Washington: GPO, 2001), p. 61.

exceeded the threshold, or measures with such costs estimated to exceed the threshold were altered prior to floor consideration to reduce their costs below the threshold.[72]

As mentioned previously, since UMRA's Title I became effective in 1996, CBO has submitted 9,397 written cost estimate statements to Congress that examined the costs imposed by provisions in a specific bill, amendment, or conference report on the private sector and state and local governments. It identified intergovernmental mandates in 1,206 of them (12.8%). CBO also reported in March 2012 that since UMRA became effective, "only 13 laws containing intergovernmental mandates with costs estimated to exceed the statutory threshold have been enacted."[73] Those laws are as follows:

- Two increases in the minimum wage—P.L. 104-188, the Small Business Job Protection Act of 1996, enacted in 1996, was estimated to cost state and local governments more than $1 billion during the first five years that it was in effect. P.L. 110-28, the U.S. Troop Readiness, Veterans' Care, Katrina Recovery, and Iraq Accountability Appropriations Act, 2007, enacted in 2007, was estimated to cost state and local governments slightly less than $1 billion during the first five years that it was in effect.

- A reduction in federal funding for administering the food stamp program, now the Supplemental Nutrition Assistance Program, P.L. 105-185, the Agricultural Research, Extension, and Education Reform Act of 1998, enacted in 1998, was estimated to cost states between $200 million and $300 million annually.

- Preemption of state taxes on premiums for certain prescription drug plans, P.L. 108-73, the Family Farmer Bankruptcy Relief Act of 2003, enacted in 2003, was estimated to cost states $70 million in revenue in 2006, the first year it was in effect, and increase to about $95 million annually by 2010.

- The temporary preemption of states' authority to tax certain Internet services and transactions, P.L. 108-435, the Internet Tax Nondiscrimination Act, enacted in 2004, was estimated to reduce state and local government tax revenue by at least $300 million; the extension of this preemption in P.L. 110-108, the Internet Tax Freedom Act Amendments Act of 2007, enacted in 2007, was estimated to reduce state and local government tax revenue by about $80 million annually.

- The requirement that state and local governments meet certain standards for issuing driver's licenses, identification cards, and vital statistics documents, P.L. 108-458, the Intelligence Reform and Terrorism Prevention Act of 2004, enacted in 2004, was estimated to cost state and local governments more than $100 million over 2005-2009, with costs exceeding the threshold in at least one of those years.

---

[72] Paul L. Posner, "Unfunded Mandates Reform Act: 1996 and Beyond," *Publius: The Journal of Federalism*, vol. 27, no. 2 (Spring 1997), pp. 57-59; U.S. General Accounting Office, *Unfunded Mandates: Analysis of Reform Act Coverage*, GAO-04-637, May 12, 2004, p. 19, at http://www.gao.gov/new.items/d04637.pdf; and U.S. Government Accountability Office, *Unfunded Mandates: Views Vary About Reform Act's Strengths, Weaknesses, and Options for Improvement*, GAO-05-454, March 31, 2005, p. 15, at http://www.gao.gov/new.items/d05454.pdf.

[73] U.S. Congressional Budget Office, *A Review of CBO's Activities in 2011 Under the Unfunded Mandates Reform Act*, March 2012, pp. 5, 45, 46, at http://www.cbo.gov/sites/default/files/cbofiles/attachments/03-30-UMRA.pdf.

- The elimination of matching federal payments for some child support spending, P.L. 109-171, the Deficit Reduction Act of 2005, enacted in 2006, was estimated to cost states more than $100 million annually beginning in 2008.

- The requirement that state and local governments withhold taxes on certain payments for property and services, P.L. 109-222, the Tax Increase Prevention and Reconciliation Act of 2005, enacted in 2006, was estimated to cost state and local governments more than $70 million annually beginning in 2011.

- Requirements on rail and transit owners and operators to train workers and submit reports to the Department of Homeland Security, P.L. 110-53, the Implementing Recommendations of the 9/11 Commission Act of 2007, enacted in 2007, was estimated to cost state and local governments more than UMRA's threshold in at least one of the first five years following enactment.

- The requirement that commuter railroads install train-control technology, P.L. 110-432, the Railroad Safety Enhancement Act of 2008, enacted in 2008, was estimated to cost state and local governments more than UMRA's threshold in at least one of the first five years following enactment.

- The requirement that public entities that handle health insurance information comply with new regulations; health insurance plans pay an annual fee based on average number of people covered by the policy; public employers pay an excise tax on employer-sponsored health insurance coverage defined as having high costs; health insurance plans comply with new standards for extending coverage; and public entities must comply with new notice and reporting requirements on health insurance plans, P.L. 111-148, the Patient Protection and Affordable Care Act, enacted in 2010, was estimated to have costs for state and local governments that would greatly exceed UMRA's thresholds in each of the first five years following enactment.

- The requirement that schools provide meals that comply with new standards for menu planning and nutrition and with nutrition standards for all food sold in schools, P.L. 111-296, the Healthy, Hunger-Free Kids Act of 2010, enacted in 2010, was estimated to have costs for state and local governments that would exceed UMRA's threshold beginning the first year that the mandates take effect.[74]

State and local government interest groups argue that these statistics confirm UMRA's effectiveness in serving as a deterrent to the enactment of new unfunded mandates that exceed UMRA's threshold and meet UMRA's definition of a federal mandate. However, they also argue that many mandates with costs below UMRA's threshold, or that do not meet UMRA's definition of a federal mandate, have been adopted since UMRA's enactment.[75]

CBO reports that from 2004 through 2011, 154 laws were enacted with at least one intergovernmental mandate as defined under UMRA. These laws imposed 284 mandates on state

---

[74] Ibid.; U.S. Congressional Budget Office, *Selected CBO Publications Related to Health Care Legislation, 2009-2010,* December 2010, pp. 17, 18, 148, 166, at http://www.cbo.gov/ftpdocs/120xx/doc12033/12-23-SelectedHealthcarePublications.pdf; and S.Rept. 111-178, Healthy, Hunger-Free Kids Act of 2010, Estimated Costs and Unfunded Mandates.

[75] National Conference of State Legislatures, "State and Federal Budgeting: Federal Mandate Relief," at http://www.ncsl.org/Default.aspx?TabID=773&tabs=855,20,632#FederalMandate.

and local governments, with 15 of these mandates exceeding UMRA's threshold, 13 with estimated costs that could not be determined, and 256 with estimated costs below the threshold. CBO also reported that hundreds of other laws had an effect on state and local government budgets, but those laws did not meet UMRA's definition of a federal mandate.[76]

As mentioned previously, CBO reported that it has submitted 9,275 cost estimate statements to Congress that examined the costs imposed by provisions in a specific bill, amendment, or conference report that might impact the private sector. It identified private-sector mandates in 1,500 of them (16.2%). CBO also reported in March 2012 that since UMRA became effective, it "has identified 116 private-sector mandates in 81 public laws with costs estimated to exceed [UMRA's] annual threshold."[77] CBO also indicated that more than half of those mandates involved taxes or fees.[78]

CBO also reports that from 2004 through 2011, 218 laws were enacted with at least one private - sector mandate as defined under UMRA. These laws imposed 490 mandates on the private sector, with 94 of these mandates exceeding UMRA's threshold, 74 with estimated costs that could not be determined, and 322 with estimated costs below the threshold.[79]

Congressional Issues for Title I

Exemptions and Exclusions

State and local government officials argue that UMRA's exemptions and exclusions reduce its effectiveness in limiting the enactment of unfunded federal intergovernmental mandates. They argue that federal programs in the exempted and excluded areas can still result in the imposition of costs on state, local, and tribal governments. Also, because UMRA does not include these costs as "mandates," they are exempt even from the requirement for CBO to estimate these costs. For example, in 2008, NCSL asserted that "although fewer than a dozen mandates have been enacted that exceed the threshold established in UMRA, Congress has shifted at least $131 billion in costs to states over the past five years" and that during the 110th Congress at least $31 billion in additional costs were imposed on states through new mandates.[80]

---

[76] U.S. Congressional Budget Office, *A Review of CBO's Activities in 2008 Under the Unfunded Mandates Reform Act*, March 2009, p. 48, at http://www.cbo.gov/ftpdocs/100xx/doc10058/03-31-UMRA.pdf; U.S. Congressional Budget Office, *A Review of CBO's Activities in 2010 Under the Unfunded Mandates Reform Act*, March 2011, p. 5, at http://www.cbo.gov/ftpdocs/121xx/doc12117/03-31-UMRA.pdf; and U.S. Congressional Budget Office, *A Review of CBO's Activities in 2011 Under the Unfunded Mandates Reform Act*, March 2012, pp. 5-7, at http://www.cbo.gov/sites/default/files/cbofiles/attachments/03-30-UMRA.pdf.

[77] U.S. Congressional Budget Office, *A Review of CBO's Activities in 2011 Under the Unfunded Mandates Reform Act*, March 2012, p. 47, at http://www.cbo.gov/sites/default/files/cbofiles/attachments/03-30-UMRA.pdf.

[78] Ibid.

[79] U.S. Congressional Budget Office, *A Review of CBO's Activities in 2008 Under the Unfunded Mandates Reform Act*, March 2009, p. 48, at http://www.cbo.gov/ftpdocs/100xx/doc10058/03-31-UMRA.pdf; U.S. Congressional Budget Office, *A Review of CBO's Activities in 2010 Under the Unfunded Mandates Reform Act*, March 2011, p. 5, at http://www.cbo.gov/ftpdocs/121xx/doc12117/03-31-UMRA.pdf; and U.S. Congressional Budget Office, *A Review of CBO's Activities in 2011 Under the Unfunded Mandates Reform Act*, March 2012, p. 8, at http://www.cbo.gov/sites/default/files/cbofiles/attachments/03-30-UMRA.pdf.

[80] National Conference of State Legislatures, *Mandate Monitor*, vol. 6, no. 1 (April 8, 2008), p. 1.

To reduce these costs, NCSL has recommended that UMRA's provisions on points of order and requirements for written cost estimate statements also apply to (1) all open-ended entitlement grant-in-aid programs, such as Medicaid, and legislative provisions that would cap or enforce a ceiling on the cost of federal participation in any entitlement or mandatory spending program; (2) new conditions of federal funding for existing federal grants and programs; (3) legislative provisions that reduce state revenues, especially when changes to the federal tax code are retroactive or otherwise provide states with little or no opportunity to prospectively address the impact of a change in federal law on state revenues; and (4) mandates that fail to exceed the statutory threshold only because they do not affect all states.[81]

For the most part, business interests have generally supported state and local government officials in their efforts to broaden UMRA's coverage of federal intergovernmental mandates. In perhaps the most extensive effort to obtain various viewpoints on UMRA, in 2005, the Government Accountability Office (GAO) held group meetings, individual interviews, and received written responses from 52 individuals and organizations, including academic centers and think tanks, businesses, federal agencies, public interest advocacy groups, and state and local governments, concerning unfunded mandates. GAO reported that UMRA's coverage was the issue most frequently commented on by parties from all five sectors, including business, and that most of the parties representing business viewed UMRA's relatively narrow coverage as a major weakness that leaves out many federal actions with potentially significant financial impacts on nonfederal parties.[82] However, GAO also found that the business sector has "generally been in favor of federal preemptions for reasons such as standardizing regulation across state and local jurisdictions."[83]

Although GAO found that most of the parties it contacted viewed UMRA's coverage of intergovernmental mandates as being too narrow, it also reported that some of the participants opposed an expansion of UMRA's coverage:

> A few parties from the public interest sector and academic/think tank sectors considered some of the existing exclusions important or identified UMRA's narrow scope as one of the act's strengths.... Specifically, these parties argued in favor of maintaining UMRA's exclusions or expanding them to include federal actions regarding public health, safety, environmental protection, workers' rights, and the disabled.... [They also] focused on the importance of the existing exclusions, particularly those dealing with constitutional and statutory rights, such as those barring discrimination against various groups.[84]

With respect to private-sector mandates in legislation, UMRA currently allows a point of order to be raised only if UMRA's informational requirements are not met; that is, only if the committee

---

[81] NCSL also advocates a revision of the definition of direct costs to capture and more accurately reflect the true costs to state governments of particular federal actions; requiring that mandate statements accompany appropriations bills; enactment of legislation that would require federal reimbursement, as long as the mandate exists, to state and local governments for costs imposed on them by any new federal mandates; restrictions regarding the preemption of state laws; repeal or modification of certain existing mandates; and a review of UMRA's existing exclusions. See, National Conference of State Legislatures, "State and Federal Budgeting: Federal Mandate Relief," at http://www.ncsl.org/Default.aspx?TabID=773&tabs=855,20,632#FederalMandate.

[82] U.S. Government Accountability Office, *Unfunded Mandates: Views Vary About Reform Act's Strengths, Weaknesses, and Options for Improvement*, GAO-05-454, March 31, 2005, p. 9, at http://www.gao.gov/new.items/d05454.pdf.

[83] Ibid., p. 12.

[84] Ibid., pp. 9, 13-14.

---

reporting the measure fails to publish a CBO cost estimate statement of the private-sector mandate's costs. Over the years, various business organizations, including the U.S. Chamber of Commerce, have advocated the extension of UMRA's substantive point of order for intergovernmental mandates to the private sector, permitting a point of order to be raised against consideration of legislation that includes private-sector mandates with costs that exceed UMRA's threshold.[85]

The GAO report also noted that "parties primarily from the academic/think tank and state and local governments sectors ... noted that while much attention has been focused on the actual (direct) costs of mandates, it is important to consider the broader implications on affected nonfederal entities beyond direct costs, including indirect costs such as opportunity costs, forgone revenues, shifting priorities, and fiscal trade-offs."[86]

During the 112th Congress, several bills were introduced to broaden UMRA's coverage. For example, H.R. 373, the Unfunded Mandates Information and Transparency Act of 2011 (as amended), and H.R. 4078, the Red Tape Reduction and Small Business Job Creation Act: Title IV, the Unfunded Mandates Information and Transparency Act of 2012, which was passed by the House on July 26, 2012, would, among other things, broaden UMRA's coverage to include assessments of indirect costs, such as foregone profits and costs passed onto consumers, as well as direct costs and, when requested by the chair or ranking Member of a committee, the prospective costs of legislation that would change conditions of federal financial assistance. These two bills, as well as H.R. 5818, the Mandate Prevention Act of 2010, would also make private-sector mandates subject to a substantive point of order. H.R. 373, H.R. 4078, S. 1189, the Unfunded Mandates Accountability Act of 2011, its companion bill in the House, H.R. 2964, and S. 1720, the Jobs Through Growth Act: Title VII, the Unfunded Mandates Accountability Act, would also remove UMRA's exemption for rules issued by most independent agencies.

UMRA and Federal Rulemaking (Title II)

UMRA's Title II, which became effective on March 22, 1995, generally requires federal agencies, unless otherwise prohibited by law, to prepare written statements that identify costs and benefits of a federal mandate to be imposed through the rulemaking process that may result in the expenditure by state, local, and tribal governments, in the aggregate, or by the private sector, of $100 million or more (adjusted annually for inflation) in any one year, before "promulgating any general notice of proposed rulemaking."[87] In 2012, the threshold for preparing a written statement is $146 million. These informational requirements for regulations, like the Title I cost estimate requirements for legislation, apply to both intergovernmental and private-sector mandates. Title II establishes no equivalent to the point of order mechanism in Title I through which either house

---

[85] U.S. Congress, Senate Committee on Government Reform, *S. 389 – The Unfunded Mandates Information Act,* hearing on S. 389, 105th Cong., 2nd sess., June 3, 1998, S.Hrg. 105-664 (Washington: GPO, 1998), pp. 28-35.

[86] U.S. Government Accountability Office, *Unfunded Mandates: Views Vary About Reform Act's Strengths, Weaknesses, and Options for Improvement,* GAO-05-454, March 31, 2005, pp. 22, 23, at http://www.gao.gov/new.items/d05454.pdf. GAO also found that "parties across the sectors suggested that various forms of retrospective analysis are needed for evaluating federal mandates after they are implemented" and "parties in the academic/think tank sector suggested analyzing the benefits of federal mandates, when appropriate, not just costs."

[87] 2 U.S.C. §1532.

can decline to consider legislation proposing covered unfunded intergovernmental mandates above the applicable threshold level.

The written assessments that federal agencies are to prepare for their regulations must identify the law authorizing the rule and include a qualitative and quantitative assessment of anticipated costs and benefits, the share of costs to be borne by the federal government, and the disproportionate budgetary effects upon particular regions, state, local, or tribal governments, or particular segments of the private sector. Assessments must also include estimates of the effect on the national economy, descriptions of consultations with nonfederal government officials, and a summary of the evaluation of comments and concerns obtained throughout the promulgation process.[88] Impacts of "any regulatory requirements" on small governments must be identified, notice must be given to those governments, and technical assistance must be provided.[89] Also, federal agencies are required, to the extent permitted in law, to develop an "effective process to permit elected officers of State, local, and tribal governments (or their designated employees with authority to act on their behalf) to provide meaningful and timely input in the development of regulatory proposals containing significant Federal intergovernmental mandates."[90] UMRA also requires federal agencies to consider "a reasonable number" of regulatory alternatives and select the "least costly, most cost-effective or least burdensome alternative" that achieves the objectives of the rule.[91]

UMRA requires the Office of Management and Budget's (OMB's) director to collect the executive branch agencies' written cost estimate statements and periodically forward copies to CBO's director. It also directs OMB to establish pilot programs in at least two federal agencies to test innovative regulatory approaches to reduce regulatory burdens on small governments, and provide Congress a written annual report detailing compliance with the act by each agency for the preceding reporting period.[92] OMB's director has delegated these responsibilities to its Office of Information and Regulatory Affairs (OIRA).

Most of these provisions were already in place when UMRA was adopted. For example, Executive Order 12866, issued in September 1993, required agencies to provide OIRA with assessments of the costs and benefits of all economically significant proposed rules (defined as having an annual impact on the economy of $100 million or more), including some rules that were not mandates; to identify regulatory alternatives and explain why the planned regulatory action is preferable to other alternatives; to issue regulations that were cost-effective and impose the least burden on society; and to seek the views of state, local, and tribal officials before imposing regulatory requirements that might significantly or uniquely affect them.[93]

---

[88] Ibid.

[89] 2 U.S.C. §1533.

[90] 2 U.S.C. §1534.

[91] 2 U.S.C. §1535.

[92] 2 U.S.C. §1536-1538. Several pilot programs were created by the EPA, including one to provide comprehensive compliance assistance to small communities and another sending faculty from schools of public administration to small communities to "minimize the adverse impact of environmental regulations on small governments." See, U.S. Office of Management and Budget, *Agency Compliance With Title I of the Unfunded Mandates Reform Act of 1995: 4th Annual Report to Congress*, October 1999, pp. 29-32, at http://www.whitehouse.gov/omb/assets/omb/inforeg/ umra1999final.pdf; and U.S. Office of Management and Budget, *Making Sense of Regulation: 2001 Report to Congress on the Costs and Benefits of Regulations and Unfunded Mandates on State, Local, and Tribal Entities*, 2001, pp. 186-188, at http://www.whitehouse.gov/sites/default/files/omb/assets/omb/inforeg/costbenefitreport.pdf.

[93] U.S. General Accounting Office, *Unfunded Mandates: Reform Act Has Had Little Effect on Agencies' Rulemaking* (continued...)

Title II's Exemptions and Exclusions

UMRA's requirement for federal agencies to issue written cost estimate statements for mandates issued through the rulemaking process that may result in expenditures of $100 million or more (adjusted annually for inflation) by state and local governments, in the aggregate, or by the private sector, in any one year, is subject to the exemptions and exclusions that apply to legislative provisions (e.g., conditions of federal assistance, duties arising from participation in a voluntary federal program, constitutional rights of individuals etc.). In addition, UMRA's requirements do not apply (1) to provisions in rules issued by independent regulatory agencies; (2) if the agency is "otherwise prohibited by law" from considering estimates of costs in adopting the rule (e.g., under the Clean Air Act the primary air quality standards are health-based and the courts have affirmed that the U.S. Environmental Protection Agency is not to consider costs in determining air quality standards for ozone and particulate matter); or (3) to any rule for which the agency does not publish a general notice of proposed rulemaking in the *Federal Register*.[94] GAO has found that about half of all final rules published in the *Federal Register* are published without a general notice of proposed rulemaking, including some rules with impacts over $100 million annually.[95]

In addition, UMRA's threshold for federal mandates in rules is limited to expenditures, in contrast to the thresholds in Title I which refer to direct costs. As a result, a federal rule's estimated annual effect on direct costs might meet Title I's threshold, but might not meet Title II's threshold if the rule does not compel nonfederal entities to spend that amount. For example, under Title I, direct costs include any amounts that state and local governments are prohibited from raising in revenue to comply with the mandate. These costs are not considered when determining whether a mandate meets Title II's threshold because funds not received are not expenditures.[96]

Also, in contrast to Title I, Title II does not require the agencies issuing regulations to address the question of whether federal funding is available to cover the costs to the private sector of mandates imposed by regulations. In general, agencies lack authority to provide such funding, which could be provided only by legislative action. Title II addresses the funding only of intergovernmental mandates, and only by requiring that agencies identify the extent to which

---

(...continued)

Actions, GAO-GDD-98-30, February 4, 1998, p. 29, at http://www.gao.gov/assets/230/225165.pdf; and U.S. Government Accountability Office, *Unfunded Mandates: Views Vary About Reform Act's Strengths, Weaknesses, and Options for Improvement*, GAO-05-454, March 31, 2005, p. 27, at http://www.gao.gov/new.items/d05454.pdf. For further analysis concerning OIRA, see CRS Report RL32397, *Federal Rulemaking: The Role of the Office of Information and Regulatory Affairs*, by Maeve P. Carey.

[94] U.S. Government Accountability Office, *Unfunded Mandates: Views Vary About Reform Act's Strengths, Weaknesses, and Options for Improvement*, GAO-05-454, March 31, 2005, pp. 26, 27, at http://www.gao.gov/new.items/d05454.pdf; and U.S. Office of Management and Budget, Office of Information and Regulatory Affairs, *2008 Report to Congress on the Benefits and Costs of Federal Regulations and Unfunded Mandates on State, Local, and Tribal Entities*, 2008, p. 25.

[95] U.S. General Accounting Office, *Federal Rulemaking: Agencies Often Published Final Actions Without Proposed Rules*, GAO/GGD-98-126, August 31, 1998, pp. 1, 2, at http://www.gao.gov/assets/230/226214.pdf; and U.S. Government Accountability Office, *Federal Rulemaking: Past Reviews and Emerging Trends Suggest Issues That Merit Congressional Attention*, GAO-06-228T, November 1, 2005, pp. 8-10, at http://www.gao.gov/assets/120/112501.pdf.

[96] U.S. Government Accountability Office, *Unfunded Mandates: Views Vary About Reform Act's Strengths, Weaknesses, and Options for Improvement*, GAO-05-454, March 31, 2005, p. 27, at http://www.gao.gov/new.items/d05454.pdf.

---

federal resources may be available to carry out those mandates.[97] The differences in the coverage of Title I and Title II may reflect a compromise reached with congressional Members who opposed using UMRA as a vehicle to address broader regulatory reform advocated by business interests. For example, Senator John Glenn argued in the Senate Committee on Governmental Affairs' committee report on UMRA:

> Another problematic change from S. 993 is the expansion of the "regulatory accountability and reform" provisions of Title 2 to go beyond intergovernmental mandates to address any and all regulatory effects on the private sector. The intended purpose of S. 1 is to control unfunded Federal mandates on State and local governments. I have always supported that goal. Moreover, I believe that if we keep the bill sharply focused on that purpose, we can get the legislation passed quickly and signed into law. If, however, we let the bill be stretched to cover other issues, we hurt prospects for enactment and we break our pledge to our friends in the State and local governments.... I believe that the bill should be brought back to its original purpose by limiting regulatory analysis to intergovernmental mandates.... In short, I support using this legislation to control intergovernmental regulatory costs. I oppose using this bill to address broader regulatory reform issues.[98]

Federal Agency Cost Estimate Statements in Major Federal Rules

From March 22, 1995, when UMRA's Title II became effective, to the end of FY2011, OMB reviewed 762 final rules with estimated benefits and/or costs exceeding $100 million annually.[99]

---

[97] 2 U.S.C. §1532 (a)(2).

[98] U.S. Congress, Senate Committee on Governmental Affairs, *Unfunded Mandate Reform Act of 1995*, report to accompany S. 1, 104th Cong., 1st sess., January 11, 1995, S.Rept. 104-1 (Washington: GPO, 1995), p. 28.

[99] U.S. General Accounting Office, *Unfunded Mandates: Reform Act Has Had Little Effect on Agencies' Rulemaking Actions*, GAO-GDD-98-30, February 4, 1998, p. 16, at http://www.gao.gov/assets/230/225165.pdf; U.S. Office of Management and Budget, *1997 Report to Congress on the Costs and Benefits of Regulations*, September 1997, chapter 3; U.S. Office of Management and Budget, *1998 Report to Congress on the Costs and Benefits of Regulations*, January 1999, p. 44; U.S. Office of Management and Budget, *2000 Report to Congress on the Costs and Benefits of Regulations*, June 2000, pp. 37, 38; U.S. Office of Management and Budget, *Making Sense of Regulation: 2001 Report to Congress on the Costs and Benefits of Regulations and Unfunded Mandates on State, Local, and Tribal Entities*, December 2001, pp. 20, 21; U.S. Office of Management and Budget, *Stimulating Smarter Regulation: 2002 Report to Congress on the Costs and Benefits of Regulations and Unfunded Mandates on State, Local, and Tribal Entities*, December 2002, pp. 46, 47; U.S. Office of Management and Budget, *Informing Regulatory Decisions: 2003 Report to Congress on the Costs and Benefits of Regulations and Unfunded Mandates on State, Local, and Tribal Entities*, September 2003, p. 10; U.S. Office of Management and Budget, *Progress in Regulatory Reform: 2004 Report to Congress on the Costs and Benefits of Regulations and Unfunded Mandates on State, Local, and Tribal Entities*, December 2004, p. 12; U.S. Office of Management and Budget, *Validating Regulatory Analysis: 2005 Report to Congress on the Costs and Benefits of Regulations and Unfunded Mandates on State, Local, and Tribal Entities*, December 2005, p. 11; U.S. Office of Management and Budget, *2006 Report to Congress on the Costs and Benefits of Regulations and Unfunded Mandates on State, Local, and Tribal Entities*, January 2007, p. 6; U.S. Office of Management and Budget, *2007 Report to Congress on the Costs and Benefits of Regulations and Unfunded Mandates on State, Local, and Tribal Entities*, June 2008, p. 7; U.S. Office of Management and Budget, *2008 Report to Congress on the Costs and Benefits of Regulations and Unfunded Mandates on State, Local, and Tribal Entities*, January 2009, p. 8; U.S. Office of Management and Budget, *Draft 2009 Report to Congress on the Benefits and Costs of Federal Regulations and Unfunded Mandates on State, Local, and Tribal Entities*, September 2009, p. 8; U.S. Office of Management and Budget, *2010 Report to Congress on the Benefits and Costs of Federal Regulations and Unfunded Mandates on State, Local, and Tribal Entities*, July 2010, p. 3; U.S. Office of Management and Budget, *2011 Report to Congress on the Benefits and Costs of Federal Regulations and Unfunded Mandates on State, Local, and Tribal Entities*, June 2011, p. 3; and U.S. Office of Management and Budget, *Draft 2012 Report to Congress on the Benefits and Costs of Federal Regulations and Unfunded Mandates on State, Local, and Tribal Entities*, March 2012, pp. 3, 32, 96.

Most (73.1%) of those "major" rules (557) did not contain provisions meeting UMRA's definition of a mandate. Whereas, as **Table 1** and **Table 2** show, CBO identified slightly more private-sector mandates than intergovernmental mandates, **Table 4** shows that most of the mandates identified in regulations have been directed at the private sector. This emphasis appears consistent with the original concern of business advocates to extend the concept of mandates to the area of regulatory reform. As indicated in **Table 4**, during the time period covered, 196 major rules met UMRA's definition of a mandate on the private sector and, therefore, were issued an UMRA cost estimate statement and 9 met UMRA's definition of a mandate on state, local, and tribal governments and, therefore, were issued an UMRA cost estimate statement.

Table 4. UMRA Written Mandate Cost Estimate Statements Issued by Federal Agencies in Final Rules, 1995-2011

Time Period	Private-Sector Mandates	Public-Sector Mandates	Total
June 1995 - May 2000	76	4	80
June 2000 - May 2001	16	2	18
May 2001 - October 2001	4	0	4
October 2001 - September 2002	5	0	5
October 2002 - September 2003	17	0	17
October 2003 - September 2004	10	0	10
October 2004 - September 2005	3	1	4
October 2005 - September 2006	9	1	10
October 2006 - September 2007	11	0	11
October 2007 - September 2008	8	0	8
October 2008 - September 2009	11	1	12
October 2009 - September 2010	13	0	13
October 2010 - September 2011	13	0	13
Total	196	9	205

Sources: Joint Hearing, U.S. Congress, House Committee on Government Reform, Subcommittee on Energy Policy, Natural Resources and Regulatory Affairs, and House Committee on Rules, Subcommittee on Technology and the House, *Unfunded Mandates: A Five Year Review and Recommendations for Change*, hearing on the Unfunded Mandates Reform Act of 1995, 107th Cong., 1st sess., May 24, 2001, H. Hrg. 107-19 (Washington: GPO, 2001), p. 40; U.S. Office of Management and Budget, *Making Sense of Regulation: 2001 Report to Congress on the Costs and Benefits of Regulations and Unfunded Mandates on State, Local, and Tribal Entities*, December 2001, pp. 189-195; U.S. Office of Management and Budget, *Stimulating Smarter Regulation: 2002 Report to Congress on the Costs and Benefits of Regulations and Unfunded Mandates on State, Local, and Tribal Entities*, December 2002, pp. 161, 162; U.S. Office of Management and Budget, *Informing Regulatory Decisions: 2003 Report to Congress on the Costs and Benefits of Regulations and Unfunded Mandates on State, Local, and Tribal Entities*, September 2003, pp. 202-204; U.S. Office of Management and Budget, *Progress in Regulatory Reform: 2004 Report to Congress on the Costs and Benefits of Regulations and Unfunded Mandates on State, Local, and Tribal Entities*, December 2004, pp. 225-234; U.S. Office of Management and Budget, *Validating Regulatory Analysis: 2005 Report to Congress on the Costs and Benefits of Regulations and Unfunded Mandates on State, Local, and Tribal Entities*, December 2005, pp. 143-148; U.S. Office of Management and Budget, *2006 Report to Congress on the Costs and Benefits of Regulations and Unfunded Mandates on State, Local, and Tribal Entities*, January 2007, pp. 141-143; U.S. Office of Management and Budget, *2007 Report to Congress on the Costs and Benefits of Regulations and Unfunded Mandates on State, Local, and Tribal Entities*, June 2008, pp. 76-81; U.S. Office of Management and Budget, *2008 Report to Congress on the Costs and Benefits of Regulations and Unfunded Mandates on State, Local, and Tribal Entities*, January 2009, pp. 77-81; U.S. Office of Management and Budget, *2009 Report to Congress on the Benefits and Costs of Federal Regulations and Unfunded Mandates on State, Local, and Tribal Entities*, January 27, 2010, pp. 62-65; U.S. Office of Management and Budget,

2010 Report to Congress on the Benefits and Costs of Federal Regulations and Unfunded Mandates on State, Local, and Tribal Entities, July 20, 2010, pp. 73-79; U.S. Office of Management and Budget, *2011 Report to Congress on the Benefits and Costs of Federal Regulations and Unfunded Mandates on State, Local, and Tribal Entities*, June 24, 2011, pp. 94-98; and U.S. Office of Management and Budget, *Draft 2012 Report to Congress on the Benefits and Costs of Federal Regulations and Unfunded Mandates on State, Local, and Tribal Entities*, March 2012, pp. 96-99.

The nine intergovernmental rules, eight issued by the U.S. Environmental Protection Agency (EPA), were as follows:

- EPA's Rule on Standards of Performance for Municipal Waste Combustors and Emissions Guidelines (1995), with estimated costs of $320 million annually;

- EPA's Standards of Performance for New Stationary Sources and Guidelines for Control of Existing Sources: Municipal Solid Waste Landfills (1996), with estimated costs of $110 million annually;

- EPA's National Primary Drinking Water Regulations: Disinfectants and Disinfection Byproducts (1998), with estimated costs of $700 million annually;

- EPA's National Primary Drinking Water Regulations: Interim Enhanced Surface Water Treatment (1998), with estimated costs of $300 million annually;

- EPA's National Pollutant Discharge Elimination: System B Regulations for Revision of the Water Pollution Control Program Addressing Storm Water Discharges (1999), with estimated costs of $803.1 million annually;

- EPA's National Primary Drinking Water Regulations; Arsenic and Clarifications to Compliance and New Source Contaminants Monitoring (2001), with estimated costs of $206 million annually;

- EPA's National Primary Drinking Water Regulations: Long Term 2 Enhanced Surface Water Treatment (2005), with estimated costs between $60 million and $170 million per year;

- EPA's National Primary Drinking Water Regulations: Stage 2 Disinfection Byproducts Rule (2006), with estimated costs of at least $100 million annually, and

- Health Insurance Reform; Modifications to the Health Insurance Portability and Accountability Act (HIPAA) Electronic Transaction Standards (2009), with estimated costs of $1.1 billion.[100]

---

[100] U.S. Office of Management and Budget, Office of Information and Regulatory Affairs, *2010 Report to Congress on the Benefits and Costs of Federal Regulations and Unfunded Mandates On State, Local, And Tribal Entities*, July 20, 2010, pp. 77, 78, at http://www.whitehouse.gov/sites/default/files/omb/legislative/reports/2010_Benefit_Cost_Report.pdf; U.S. Office of Management and Budget, Office of Information and Regulatory Affairs, *2008 Report to Congress on the Benefits and Costs of Federal Regulations and Unfunded Mandates on State, Local, and Tribal Entities*, 2009, pp. 24-27, at http://www.whitehouse.gov/sites/default/files/omb/assets/information_and_regulatory_affairs/2008_cb_final.pdf; and U.S. Office of Management and Budget, *2000 Report to Congress On the Costs and Benefits of Federal Regulations*, p. 31, at http://www.whitehouse.gov/omb/assets/omb/inforeg/2000fedreg-report.pdf. The rule on Standards for Privacy of Individually Available Health Information, issued in 2001 by the Department of Health and Human Services, was identified as costing state and local governments $240 million annually, but the rule was later determined not to be an enforceable duty as defined under UMRA. The Department of Homeland Security's (DHS) Chemical Facility Anti-Terrorism Standards Rule, issued in 2007, was identified as having the potential to require certain municipalities that own and/or operate power generating facilities to purchase security enhancements. However, DHS was unable to determine whether the rule would impose an (continued...)

Impact on the Rulemaking Process

In 1997, Senators Fred Thompson and John Glenn, chair and ranking minority Member of the Senate Committee on Governmental Affairs, respectively, asked GAO to review federal agencies' implementation of UMRA's Title II. On February 4, 1998, GAO issued its report, concluding that "our review of federal agencies' implementation of Title II of UMRA indicates that this title of the act has had little direct effect on agencies' rulemaking actions during the first 2 years of its implementation."[101]

GAO concluded that Title II had limited impact on agencies' rulemaking primarily because of its limited coverage. For example, GAO noted that written mandate cost estimate statements were not on file at CBO for 80 of the 110 economically significant rules published in the *Federal Register* between March 22, 1995 and March 22, 1997. GAO examined the 80 economically significant rules that lacked a written mandate cost estimate statement and concluded that UMRA did not require a written mandate cost estimate statement for 78 of them because the rule either did not have an associated notice of proposed rulemaking (18 instances); did not impose an enforceable duty (3 instances); imposed such a duty but only as a condition of federal assistance (33 instances); imposed such a duty but only as part of a voluntary program (11 instances); did not involve an expenditure of $100 million in any single year by the private sector or by state, local, and tribal governments (12 instances); or incorporated requirements specifically set forth in law (one instance). GAO concluded that written mandate cost estimate statements should have been filed at CBO for two of the rules that lacked one, but, in both instances, the rules appeared to satisfy UMRA's written statement requirements.[102]

Even where UMRA applied, GAO concluded that the act did not appear to have had much effect on federal agencies' rulemaking actions because UMRA does not require agencies to take the actions required in the statute if the agencies determine that the actions are duplicative of other actions or that accurate estimates of the rule's future compliance costs are not feasible.[103] Because federal agencies' rules commonly contain an estimate of compliance costs, GAO found that most agencies rarely prepared a separate UMRA written cost estimate statement. Moreover, Executive Order 12866, which was issued more than a year before UMRA's enactment, already required federal agencies to provide OIRA with assessments of the costs and benefits of all economically significant rules. GAO also concluded that UMRA did not substantially change agencies' intergovernmental consultation processes.[104]

In 2001, OMB's director, Mitchell L. Daniels, Jr., acknowledged at a House hearing coinciding with UMRA's fifth anniversary that UMRA's Title II had not resulted in major changes in federal agency rulemaking. He noted that, according to OMB's five annual reports to Congress on the implementation of Title II, 80 rules had required the preparation of a separate written mandate

---

(...continued)

enforceable duty on state and local governments of $100 million or more (adjusted for inflation) in any one year. OMB includes the rule as a state and local government mandate meeting UMRA's requirements "for the sake of completeness."

[101] U.S. General Accounting Office, *Unfunded Mandates: Reform Act Has Had Little Effect on Agencies' Rulemaking Actions*, GAO-GDD-98-30, February 4, 1998, p. 29, at http://www.gao.gov/assets/230/225165.pdf.

[102] Ibid., pp. 12-16.

[103] Ibid., p. 28.

[104] Ibid., pp. 21, 22.

cost estimate statement (see **Table 4**). He said that "it was hard to believe that only 80 regulations had significant impacts on state, local, or tribal governments, or the private sector. In fact, it appears that agencies have attempted to limit their consultative processes, and ignored potential alternative remedies, by aggressively utilizing the exemptions outlined by the Act."[105] He added that "when agencies fail to solicit or consider the views of states and localities, they deny themselves the benefit of state and local innovation and experience. This will not be accepted practice in this [George W. Bush] Administration."[106]

In 2004, GAO released a second study of UMRA's implementation of Title II (and the first for Title I), focusing on statutes enacted and rules published during 2001 and 2002. GAO found that 5 of 377 statutes enacted and 9 of 122 major or economically significant final rules issued in 2001 or 2002 were identified as containing federal mandates at or above UMRA's thresholds.[107] GAO concluded its report by stating that "the findings raise the question of whether UMRA's procedures, definitions, and exclusions adequately capture and subject to scrutiny federal statutory and regulatory actions that might impose significant financial burdens on affected nonfederal parties."[108]

As noted earlier, in 2005, GAO sought and received input from participating parties about UMRA's strengths and weaknesses and potential options for reinforcing the strengths or addressing the weaknesses. It also held a symposium on federal mandates to examine those identified strengths and weaknesses in more depth.[109] Although the symposium's participants viewed UMRA's coverage as its most significant issue, GAO reported that comments received concerning federal agency consultation with state and local governments under Title II "focused on the quality of consultations across agencies, which was viewed as inconsistent" and that "a few parties commented that UMRA had improved consultation and collaboration between federal agencies and nonfederal levels of government."[110]

At a Senate hearing held on April 14, 2005, OIRA's director, John Graham, testified that OMB includes summaries of agency consultations with state and local government officials in its annual report to Congress and that "this year's report shows an increased level of engagement."[111] He added that there were "some very good examples of consultation that are documented in that report at the Department of Education, the Environmental Protection Agency and so forth, but I think that it would be fair to say that those best practices are not necessarily uniform across the

---

[105] Joint Hearing, U.S. Congress, House Committee on Government Reform, Subcommittee on Energy Policy, Natural Resources and Regulatory Affairs, and House Committee on Rules, Subcommittee on Technology and the House, *Unfunded Mandates: A Five Year Review and Recommendations for Change*, hearing on the Unfunded Mandates Reform Act of 1995, 107th Cong., 1st sess., May 24, 2001, H. Hrg. 107-19 (Washington: GPO, 2001), p. 40.

[106] Ibid.

[107] U.S. General Accounting Office, *Unfunded Mandates: Analysis of Reform Act Coverage*, GAO-04-637, May 12, 2004, pp. 4, 28-33, at http://www.gao.gov/new.items/d04637.pdf.

[108] Ibid., pp. 36, 37.

[109] U.S. Government Accountability Office, *Unfunded Mandates: Views Vary About Reform Act's Strengths, Weaknesses, and Options for Improvement*, GAO-05-454, March 31, 2005, pp. 3, 4, at http://www.gao.gov/new.items/d05454.pdf.

[110] Ibid., p. 20.

[111] U.S. Congress, Senate Committee on Homeland Security and Governmental Affairs, Subcommittee on Oversight of Government Management, the Federal Workforce, and the District of Columbia, *Passing the Buck: A Review of the Unfunded Mandates Reform Act*, hearing on the Unfunded Mandates Reform Act, 109th Cong., 1st sess., April 14, 2005, S. Hrg. 109-82 (Washington: GPO, 2005), p. 52.

federal government or across any particular agency."[112] State and local government officials testifying at the hearing stated that federal agency consultation had improved somewhat, but remained "sporadic."[113]

Congressional Issues for Title II

Exemptions and Exclusions

State and local government public interest groups continue to advocate a broadening of Title II's coverage. For example, as mentioned previously, they advocate a broader definition of what UMRA considers a mandate, under the presumption that a broader definition would subject more rules to Title II. An alternative approach would be to separate debates concerning the definition of "mandate" and UMRA's coverage, and, instead, apply Title II's information requirements to whatever classes of federally induced costs Congress deems appropriate to cover. This approach might be implemented by incorporating coverage of various kinds of "federally induced costs," adopting the terminology proposed earlier by ACIR. In either case, inasmuch as Title II's requirements are informational only, their extension to new classes of regulations, or to new kinds of federally induced costs, would not affect the authority of agencies to issue regulations or the substance of the regulations that could be issued.

As mentioned previously, UMRA's threshold for federal mandates in rules is limited to expenditures, in contrast to the thresholds in Title I that refer to direct costs. Several bills were introduced during the 112th Congress to broaden Title II's coverage. For example, S. 1189, the Unfunded Mandates Accountability Act of 2011, its companion bill in the House, H.R. 2964, and S. 1720, the Jobs Through Growth Act: Title VII, the Unfunded Mandates Accountability Act, would also remove UMRA's exemption for rules issued by most independent agencies. These bills would, among other things, also amend Title II to apply to "the cost of compliance and any reasonably foreseeable indirect costs, including revenues lost as a result of an agency rule subject to this section."[114] The bills would also require each federal agency to prepare and publish in the *Federal Register* an initial and final regulatory impact analysis and, before promulgating any proposed or final rule for which a regulatory impact analysis is required, identify and consider a reasonable number of regulatory alternatives and select the least costly, most cost-effective, or least burdensome alternative that achieves the statute's objectives.[115]

---

[112] Ibid., pp. 16.

[113] Ibid., pp. 22, 23, 27.

[114] S. 1189, the Unfunded Mandates Accountability Act of 2011, §202. Regulatory Impact Analyses For Certain Rules. The bill was referred to the Senate Committee on Homeland Security and Governmental Affairs. H.R. 2964, the Unfunded Mandates Accountability Act of 2011, §202. Regulatory Impact Analyses For Certain Rules. The bill was referred to the House Committee on Oversight and Government Reform's Subcommittee on Technology, Information Policy, Intergovernmental Relations and Procurement Reform and to the House Committee on the Judiciary, the House Committee on Rules, and the House Committee on the Budget. S. 1720, the Jobs Through Growth Act: Title VII, the Unfunded Mandates Accountability Act, §3703. Regulatory Impact Analyses For Certain Rules. The bill was placed on Senate Legislative Calendar under General Orders.

[115] S. 1189, the Unfunded Mandates Accountability Act of 2011, §205. Least Burdensome Option or Explanation Required; S. 1720, the Jobs Through Growth Act §3704. Least burdensome option or explanation required; and H.R. 2964, the Unfunded Mandates Accountability Act of 2011, §205. Least Burdensome Option or Explanation Required; and S. 1720, the Jobs Through Growth Act: Title VII, the Unfunded Mandates Accountability Act, §3704. Least Burdensome Option or Explanation Required.

State and local government advocacy groups have also argued that Title II should apply to rules issued by independent regulatory agencies.[116] Although OMB does not review rules issued by independent regulatory agencies, in recent years it has included information concerning independent regulatory agency rules in its annual UMRA report to Congress. According to those reports, independent regulatory agencies issued 185 major rules from FY1997 through FY2011.[117] S. 1189, S. 1720, and H.R. 2964 would, among other things, amend Title II to apply to rules issued by most independent regulatory agencies. The bills would retain the exemption for rules that concern monetary policy proposed or implemented by the Board of Governors of the Federal Reserve System or the Federal Open Market Committee.[118]

The National Association of Counties (NACO) and other state and local government public interest groups have also advocated a strengthening of OMB's role in the enforcement of Title II to ensure consistent application of UMRA's provisions across federal agencies.[119] For example, NCSL's current policy statement on unfunded mandates recommends that UMRA be amended to include "the creation of an office within the Office of Management and Budget that is analogous to the State and Local Government Cost Estimates Unit at the Congressional Budget Office."[120] Business organizations, led by the U.S. Chamber of Commerce, also have advocated an independent review of federal agency cost estimates, recommending that the reviews be conducted by OMB or GAO. They also have advocated the permitting of early judicial challenges to an agency's failure to complete an UMRA cost estimate statement or for completing one that is deficient.[121]

H.R. 214, the Congressional Office of Regulatory Analysis Creation and Sunset and Review Act of 2011, would create a Congressional Office of Regulatory Analysis.[122] The bill includes a

---

[116] U.S. Congress, Senate Committee on Homeland Security and Governmental Affairs, Subcommittee on Oversight of Government Management, the Federal Workforce, and the District of Columbia, *Passing the Buck: A Review of the Unfunded Mandates Reform Act*, hearing on the Unfunded Mandates Reform Act, 109th Cong., 1st sess., April 14, 2005, S. Hrg. 109-82 (Washington: GPO, 2005), pp. 112-126, 167-174.

[117] U.S. Office of Management and Budget, *2007 Report to Congress on the Costs and Benefits of Regulations and Unfunded Mandates on State, Local, and Tribal Entities*, June 2008, p. 16; U.S. Office of Management and Budget, *2011 Report to Congress on the Benefits and Costs of Federal Regulations and Unfunded Mandates on State, Local, and Tribal Entities*, June 24, 2011, p. 4; and U.S. Office of Management and Budget, *Draft 2012 Report to Congress on the Benefits and Costs of Federal Regulations and Unfunded Mandates on State, Local, and Tribal Entities*, March , 2012, p. 122.

[118] S. 1189, the Unfunded Mandates Accountability Act of 2011, its companion bill in the House, H.R. 2964, and S. 1720, the Jobs Through Growth Act: Title VII, the Unfunded Mandates Accountability Act, include several provisions concerning UMRA. Previously, S. 817, to provide for the inclusion of independent regulatory agencies in the application of the Unfunded Mandates Reform Act of 1995, was introduced on April 14, 2011. The bill applied only to UMRA's exemption of independent regulatory agencies.

[119] U.S. Congress, Senate Committee on Homeland Security and Governmental Affairs, Subcommittee on Oversight of Government Management, the Federal Workforce, and the District of Columbia, *Passing the Buck: A Review of the Unfunded Mandates Reform Act*, hearing on the Unfunded Mandates Reform Act, 109th Cong., 1st sess., April 14, 2005, S. Hrg. 109-82 (Washington: GPO, 2005), p. 124.

[120] National Conference of State Legislatures, "State and Federal Budgeting: Federal Mandate Relief," at http://www.ncsl.org/Default.aspx?TabID=773&tabs=855,20,632#FederalMandate.

[121] Joint Hearing, U.S. Congress, House Committee on Government Reform, Subcommittee on Energy Policy, Natural Resources and Regulatory Affairs, and House Committee on Rules, Subcommittee on Technology and the House, *Unfunded Mandates: A Five Year Review and Recommendations for Change*, hearing on the Unfunded Mandates Reform Act of 1995, 107th Cong., 1st sess., May 24, 2001, H. Hrg. 107-19 (Washington: GPO, 2001), pp. 80, 88, 89.

[122] H.R. 214, the Congressional Office of Regulatory Analysis Creation and Sunset and Review Act of 2011, was introduced on January 7, 2011 and referred to the House Committee on the Judiciary and House Committee on Oversight and Government Reform. The bill was later referred to the House Committee on the Judiciary's (continued...)

---

provision that would transfer from CBO's director to the director of the proposed Congressional Office of Regulatory Analysis the responsibility to compare federal agency estimates of the cost of regulations implementing an act containing a federal mandate to the CBO's estimate of those costs. The Congressional Office of Regulatory Analysis would also receive federal agency statements that accompany significant regulatory actions.

As mentioned previously, organizations representing various environmental and social groups have argued that UMRA has achieved its stated goals of strengthening the partnership between the federal government and state, local, and tribal governments by promoting informed and deliberate decisions by Congress on the appropriateness of federal mandates. In their view, broadening UMRA's coverage would dilute its impact. For example, a participant at GAO's 2005 symposium on federal mandates argued that eliminating any of UMRA's exclusions and exemptions might make the identification of mandates less meaningful, saying "The more red flags run up, the less important the red flag becomes."[123] Also, some of the participants at the symposium from the academic, policy research institute, and public interest advocacy sectors argued that it was essential that some of the existing exclusions, such as those dealing with constitutional and statutory rights barring discrimination against various groups, be retained. They also advocated additional exclusions to include federal actions regarding public health, safety, environmental protection, workers' rights, and the disabled.[124]

Federal Agency Consultation Requirements

State and local government public interest groups assert that enhanced requirements for federal agency consultation with state and local government officials during the rulemaking process are needed.[125] For example, the NCSL has asserted that federal agency "consultation with state and local governments in the construction of these rules is haphazard."[126] It recommends that Title II be amended to include "enhanced requirements for federal agencies to consult with state and local governments."[127]

OMB asserts that "federal agencies have been actively consulting with states, localities, and tribal governments in order to ensure that regulatory activities were conducted consistent with the requirements of UMRA."[128] In addition, OMB notes that it has had guidelines in place since September 21, 1995, to assist federal agencies in complying with the act.[129] The current

---

(...continued)

Subcommittee on Courts, Commercial and Administrative Law and the House Committee on Oversight and Government Reform's Subcommittee on Regulatory Affairs, Stimulus Oversight and Government Spending.

[123] U.S. Government Accountability Office, *Unfunded Mandates: Views Vary About Reform Act's Strengths, Weaknesses, and Options for Improvement*, GAO-05-454, March 31, 2005, p. 13, at http://www.gao.gov/new.items/d05454.pdf.

[124] Ibid.

[125] National Conference of State Legislatures, "State and Federal Budgeting: Federal Mandate Relief," at http://www.ncsl.org/Default.aspx?TabID=773&tabs=855,20,632#FederalMandate.

[126] National Conference of State Legislatures, "Policy Position on Federal Mandate Relief," effective through August 2011.

[127] National Conference of State Legislatures, "State and Federal Budgeting: Federal Mandate Relief," at http://www.ncsl.org/Default.aspx?TabID=773&tabs=855,20,632#FederalMandate.

[128] U.S. Office of Management and Budget, *2011 Report to Congress on the Benefits and Costs of Federal Regulations and Unfunded Mandates on State, Local, and Tribal Entities*, June 24, 2011, p. 93.

[129] U.S. Office of Management and Budget, *Agency Compliance with Title II of the Unfunded Mandates Reform Act of* (continued...)

---

guidelines suggest that (1) intergovernmental consultations should take place as early as possible, beginning before issuance of a proposed rule and continuing through the final rule stage, and be integrated explicitly into the rulemaking process; (2) agencies should consult with a wide variety of state, local, and tribal officials; (3) agencies should estimate direct benefits and costs to assist with these consultations; (4) the scope of consultation should reflect the cost and significance of the mandate being considered; (5) effective consultation requires trust and significant and sustained attention so that all who participate can enjoy frank discussion and focus on key priorities; and (6) agencies should seek out state, local, and tribal views on costs, benefits, risks, and alternative methods of compliance, and whether the federal rule will harmonize with and not duplicate similar laws in other levels of government.[130]

OMB often includes summaries of selected consultation activities by agencies whose actions affect state, local, and tribal governments in its annual draft and final UMRA reports to Congress. OMB has argued that the summaries are an indication that federal agencies are complying with the act. For example, in OMB's draft 2012 UMRA report to Congress, OMB wrote in the introduction to these summaries:

> Four agencies (the Departments of Agriculture, Commerce, Energy, and Health and Human Services) have provided examples of consultation activities that involved State, local and tribal governments not only in their regulatory processes, but also in their program planning and implementation phases. These agencies have worked to enhance the regulatory environment by improving the way in which the Federal Government relates to its intergovernmental partners. In general, many of the departments and agencies not listed here (including the Departments of Justice, State, Treasury, and Veterans Affairs, the Small Business Administration, and the General Services Administration) do not often impose mandates upon States, localities or tribes, and thus have fewer occasions to consult with these governments.
>
> As the following descriptions indicate, Federal agencies conduct a wide range of consultations. Agency consultations sometimes involve multiple levels of government, depending on the agency's understanding of the scope and impact of the rule. OMB continues to work with agencies to ensure that consultation occurs with the appropriate level of government.[131]

During the 112th Congress, several bills were introduced which would require federal agencies to enhance their consultation with UMRA stakeholders, including H.R. 373, the Unfunded Mandates Information and Transparency Act of 2011, and H.R. 4078, the Red Tape Reduction and Small Business Job Creation Act: Title IV, the Unfunded Mandates Information and Transparency Act of 2012, which the House passed on July 26, 2012.[132]

(...continued)

1995: 4th Annual Report to Congress from the Director of the Office of Management and Budget, October 1999, p. 2.

[130] U.S. Office of Management and Budget, *2008 Report to Congress on the Costs and Benefits of Regulations and Unfunded Mandates on State, Local, and Tribal Entities*, January 2009, pp. 75, 76.

[131] U.S. Office of Management and Budget, *Draft 2012 Report to Congress on the Benefits and Costs of Federal Regulations and Unfunded Mandates on State, Local, and Tribal Entities*, March 2012, p. 158.

[132] H.R. 373, the Unfunded Mandates Information and Transparency Act of 2011, §10. Enhanced stakeholder consultation; and H.R. 4078, the Red Tape Reduction and Small Business Job Creation Act: Title IV, the Unfunded Mandates Information and Transparency Act of 2012-, §410. Enhanced stakeholder consultation.

Concluding Observations

In 1995, UMRA's enactment was considered an historic, milestone event in the history of American intergovernmental relations. For example, when signing UMRA, President Bill Clinton said,

> Today, we are making history. We are working to find the right balance for the 21st century. We are recognizing that the pendulum had swung too far, and that we have to rely on the initiative, the creativity, the determination, and the decisionmaking of people at the State and local level to carry much of the load for America as we move into the 21st century.[133]

Since UMRA's enactment, parties participating in its implementation and researchers in the academic community, policy research institutes, and nonpartisan government agencies have reached different conclusions concerning the extent of UMRA's impact on intergovernmental relations and whether UMRA should be amended. State and local government officials and federalism scholars generally view UMRA as having a limited, though positive, impact on intergovernmental relations. In their view, the federal government has continued to expand its authority through the "carrots" of increased federal assistance and the "sticks" of grant conditions, preemptions, mandates, and administrative rulemaking. Facing what they view as a seemingly ever growing federal influence in American governance, they generally advocate a broadening of UMRA's coverage to enhance its impact, emphasizing the need to include conditions of grant assistance and a broader range of federal agency rulemaking, including rules issued by independent regulatory agencies.

Other organizations, representing various environmental and social groups, argue that UMRA's coverage does not need to be broadened. In their view, UMRA has accomplished its goals of fostering improved intergovernmental relations and ensuring that when Congress votes on major federal mandates it is aware of the costs imposed by the legislation. They assert that UMRA's current limits on coverage should be maintained or reinforced by adding exclusions for mandates regarding public health, safety, workers' rights, environmental protection, and the disabled.[134]

During the 111th Congress, UMRA received increased attention as Congress considered various proposals to reform health care. Governors, for example, expressed opposition to proposals that would have required states to contribute toward the cost of expanding Medicaid eligibility, asserting that the expansion could inflate state deficits and impose on states what Tennessee Governor Philip Bredesen reportedly described as the "mother of all unfunded mandates."[135] However, as mentioned previously, proposals to expand Medicaid eligibility are not covered by UMRA because it has been determined that states "have significant flexibility to make

---

[133] President Bill Clinton, "Remarks on Signing the Unfunded Mandates Reform Act of 1995," *Weekly Compilation of Presidential Documents*, vol. 31, no. 12 (March 22, 1995), p. 455.

[134] U.S. Government Accountability Office, *Unfunded Mandates: Views Vary About Reform Act's Strengths, Weaknesses, and Options for Improvement*, GAO-05-454, March 31, 2005, pp. 5-7, 9-14, at http://www.gao.gov/ new.items/d05454.pdf.

[135] Robert Pear and David M. Herszenhorn, "Senators Hear Concerns Over Costs of Health Proposal," *The New York Times*, August 6, 2009, at http://www.nytimes.com/2009/08/07/health/policy/07health.html?hpw; Clifford Krauss, Governors Fear Added Costs in Health Care Overhaul, *The New York Times*, August 6, 2009, at http://www.nytimes.com/2009/08/07/business/07medicaid.html; and Chas Sisk, "Tennessee Gov. Bredesen takes lead role in fight over health costs," *The Tennessean*, August 18, 2009, at http://www.tennessean.com/article/20090818/ NEWS02/908180357/1009/NEWS02/Tennessee+Gov.+Bredesen+takes+lead+role+in+fight+over+health+costs.

---

programmatic adjustments in their Medicaid programs to accommodate" new federal requirements.[136]

As discussed previously, during the 112th Congress several bills were introduced, and one bill was passed by the House (H.R. 4078, the Red Tape Reduction and Small Business Job Creation Act: Title IV, the Unfunded Mandates Information and Transparency Act of 2012), that would broaden UMRA's coverage. For example, H.R. 4078 would, among other provisions,

- require CBO to assess the prospective costs of changes in conditions of federal financial assistance when requested by the chair or ranking Member of a committee;

- broaden UMRA's coverage to include assessments of indirect as well as direct costs by amending the definition of direct costs to include forgone profits, costs passed onto consumers or other entities, and, to the extent practicable, behavioral changes;

- expand the scope of reporting requirements to include regulations imposed by independent regulatory agencies;

- make private-sector mandates subject to a substantive point of order;

- establish principals for federal agencies to follow when assessing the effects of regulations on state and local governments and the private sector, including requiring the agency to identify the problem it seeks to address, determining whether existing laws or regulations could be modified to address the problem, identifying alternatives, and designing its regulations in the most cost-effective manner available;

- expand the scope of cost statements accompanying significant regulatory actions to include, among other requirements, a reasonably detailed description of the need for the proposed rulemaking or final rule and an explanation of how the proposed rulemaking or final rule will meet that need; an assessment of the potential costs and benefits of the proposed rulemaking or final rule; estimates of the mandate's future compliance costs and any disproportionate budgetary effects upon any particular regions of the nation or state, local, or tribal governments; a detailed description of the agency's consultation with the private sector or elected representatives of the affected state, local, or tribal governments; and a detailed summary of how the agency complied with each of the regulatory principles included in the bill;

- require federal agencies to meet enhanced levels of consultation with state, local, and tribal governments and the private sector before issuing a notice of proposed rulemaking or a final rule; and

- require federal agencies to conduct a retrospective analysis of the costs and benefits of an existing regulation when requested by the chair or ranking Member of a committee.[137]

---

[136] U.S. Congressional Budget Office, "Cost Estimate for the Patient Protection and Affordable Care Act," November 18, 2009, p. 18, at http://www.cbo.gov/ftpdocs/107xx/doc10731/Reid_letter_11_18_09.pdf.

[137] H.R. 4078, the Red Tape Reduction and Small Business Job Creation Act: Title IV, the Unfunded Mandates Information and Transparency Act of 2012, was passed by the House on July 26, 2012, and placed on Senate legislative (continued...)

Underlying disagreements over UMRA's future are fundamentally different values concerning American federalism. One view emphasizes the importance of freeing state and local government officials from the constraints brought about by the directives and costs associated with federal mandates so they can experiment with innovative ways to achieve results with greater efficiency and cost effectiveness. This view focuses on the positive effect active state and local governments can have in promoting a sense of state and community responsibility and self-reliance, encouraging participation and civic responsibility by allowing more people to become involved in public questions, adapting public programs to state and local needs and conditions, and reducing the political turmoil that sometimes results from single policies that govern the entire nation.[138]

Another view emphasizes the federal government's responsibility to ensure that all citizens are afforded minimum levels of essential government services. This view focuses on the propensity of states to restrict governmental services because they compete with one another for businesses and taxpaying residents; the variation in state fiscal capacities that make it difficult for some states to provide certain governmental services even though they might have the political will to do so; and the propensity of states to have different views concerning what services are essential and what constitutes a sufficient level of essential government services.[139]

Given these disagreements over fundamental values, it is perhaps not surprising that there are differences of opinion concerning UMRA's future. Using President Clinton's words, debates over UMRA's future are more than just arguments over who will pay for what; they are also about finding "the right balance" for American federalism in the 21st century.

(...continued)

calendar under general orders on July 31, 2012. No further action has taken place on the bill. Title IV included language from H.R. 373, the Unfunded Mandates Information and Transparency Act of 2011 (as amended).

[138] Thomas R. Dye, *Understanding Public Policy*, 6th edition (Englewood Cliffs, N.J.: Prentice-Hall, Inc., 1987), p. 301.

[139] Ibid., p. 300; ACIR, *Categorical Grants: Their Role and Design* (Washington, DC: ACIR, 1978), pp. 50-58; and Claude E. Barfield, *Rethinking Federalism: Block Grants and Federal, State, and Local Responsibilities* (Washington, DC: American Enterprise Institute, 1981), pp. 4-8.

Appendix A. The Rise of Unfunded Mandates as a National Issue and UMRA's Legislative History

Unfunded mandates became a national issue during the 1980s as state and local government officials and their affiliated public interest groups, led by the National League of Cities (NLC), U.S. Conference of Mayors (USCM), and National Association of Counties (NACO), began an intensive lobbying effort to limit unfunded intergovernmental mandates. Their efforts were supported by various business organizations, led by the U.S. Chamber of Commerce, which opposed the imposition of unfunded mandates on both state and local governments and the private sector, particularly mandates issued through federal rules.[140]

Increased Number and Cost of Unfunded Mandates

State and local government officials became involved in the issue of unfunded federal mandates during the 1980s primarily because the number and costs of unfunded intergovernmental mandates were increasing and, by then, nearly every community in the nation had become subject to their effects. For example, ACIR reported that during the 1980s the costs of unfunded intergovernmental mandates were increasing at a rate faster than federal assistance. ACIR also identified 63 federal statutes as of 1990 that, in its view, imposed "major" restrictions or costs on state and local governments. Many of the statutes involved civil rights, consumer protection, improved health and safety, and environmental protection.[141] Only two of the 63 statutes it identified, the Davis-Bacon Act of 1931 and Hatch Act of 1940, were enacted prior to 1964, 9 were enacted during the 1960s, 25 during the 1970s, 21 during the 1980s, and 6 in 1990. A study completed by the Clinton Administration's National Performance Review identified 172 laws in force that imposed requirements (regardless of the magnitude of their impact) on state and local governments as of December 1992.[142]

Some of the major federal statutes adopted during the 1970s that imposed relatively costly federal mandates on state and local governments were the Equal Employment Opportunity Act of 1972, which extended the prohibitions against discrimination in employment contained in the Civil Rights Act of 1964 to state and local government employment; the Fair Labor Standards Act Amendments of 1974, which extended the prohibitions against age discrimination in the Age Discrimination in Employment Act of 1967 to state and local government employment; and the Public Utilities Regulatory Policy Act of 1978, which established federal requirements

---

[140] Vernon Louviere, "The Strings Become a Noose," *Nation's Business*, vol. 69, no. 3 (March 1981), p. 64; Joan C. Szabo, "How Costly are Mandated Benefits?" *Nation's Business*, vol. 76, no. 4 (April 1988), p. 14; Mary McElvenn, "The Federal Impact on Business," *Nation's Business*, vol. 79, no. 1 (January 1991), pp. 23-26; David Warner, "Regulations' Staggering Costs," *Nation's Business*, vol. 80, no. 6 (June 1992), pp. 50-53; Michael Barrier, "Taxing the Man Behind the Tree," *Nation's Business*, vol. 81, no. 9 (September 1993), pp. 31, 32; and Michael Barrier, "Mandates Foes Smell a Victory," *Nation's Business*, vol. 82, no. 9 (September 1994), p. 50.

[141] ACIR, *Regulatory Federalism: Policy, Process, Impact, and Reform*, A-95 (Washington, DC: ACIR, 1984), pp. 19-21; and ACIR, *Federal Regulation of State and Local Governments: The Mixed Record of the 1980s*, A-126 (Washington, DC: ACIR, 1993), pp. 44, 45.

[142] Office of the Vice-President, *Strengthening the Partnership in Intergovernmental Service Delivery, National Performance Review Accompanying Report* (Washington, DC: GPO, September 1993), http://govinfo.library.unt.edu/npr/library/reports/isd.html.

---

concerning the pricing of electricity and natural gas.[143] One of the more costly federal mandates enacted during the 1970s was Section 504 of the Rehabilitation Act of 1973. It prohibited discrimination against handicapped persons in federally assisted programs. CBO estimated that it would require states and localities to spend $6.8 billion over 30 years to equip buses with wheelchair lifts, to install elevators in subway systems, and to expand access to public transit systems for the physically disabled.[144]

Three of the more costly unfunded federal mandates adopted during the 1980s were the Safe Drinking Water Act Amendments of 1986 (which was estimated to impose an additional cost of between $2 billion and $3 billion on state and local governments to improve public water systems); the Asbestos Hazard Emergency Response Act of 1986 (which required schools to remove hazardous asbestos at an estimated cost of $3.15 billion over 30 years); and the Water Quality Act of 1987 (which was estimated to cost states and localities about $12 billion in capital costs for wastewater treatment).[145] ACIR estimated that new federal mandates adopted between 1983 and 1990 cost state and local governments between $8.9 billion and $12.7 billion, depending on the definition of mandate used; in FY1991, federal mandates imposed estimated costs of between $2.2 billion and $3.6 billion on state and local governments; and additional mandates, not included in these estimates, were scheduled to take effect in the years ahead.[146]

ACIR suggested that the expansion of federal intergovernmental mandates during the 1960s, 1970s, and 1980s fundamentally changed the nature of intergovernmental relations in the United States:

> During the 1960s and 1970s, state and local governments for the first time were brought under extensive federal regulatory controls.... Over this period, national controls have been adopted affecting public functions and services ranging from automobile inspection, animal preservation and college athletics to waste treatment and waste disposal. In field after field the power to set standards and determine methods of compliance has shifted from the states and localities to Washington.[147]

State and Local Governments Seek Relief from Unfunded Mandates

Edward I. Koch, then mayor of New York City and a former Member of Congress, was one of the first public officials to highlight the mandate issue. In 1980, he authored an article criticizing what he called "the mandate millstone."[148] He noted that as a Member of Congress he voted for many federal mandates "with every confidence that we were enacting sensible permanent solutions to critical problems" but now that he was a mayor he had come to realize that "over the

---

[143] ACIR, *Regulatory Federalism: Policy, Process, Impact, and Reform*, A-95 (Washington, DC: ACIR, 1984), p. 88.

[144] ACIR, *Federal Regulation of State and Local Governments: The Mixed Record of the 1980s*, A-126 (Washington, DC: ACIR, 1993), p. 61.

[145] Ibid., p. 46; and Timothy J. Conlan and David R. Beam, "Federal Mandates: The Record of Reform and Future Prospects," *Intergovernmental Perspective*, vol. 18, no. 4 (Fall 1992), pp. 9, 10.

[146] Timothy J. Conlan and David R. Beam, "Federal Mandates: The Record of Reform and Future Prospects," *Intergovernmental Perspective*, vol. 18, no. 4 (Fall 1992), pp. 9, 10.

[147] ACIR, *Regulatory Federalism: Policy, Process, Impact, and Reform*, A-95 (Washington, DC: ACIR, 1984), p. 246.

[148] Edward I. Koch, "The Mandate Millstone," *The Public Interest*, no. 61 (Fall 1980), pp. 42-57.

past decade, a maze of complex statutory and administrative directives has come to threaten both the initiative and the financial health of local governments throughout the country."[149]

The continued growth in the number and cost of federal mandates during the 1980s and early 1990s generated renewed and heightened opposition from state and local government officials and their affiliated public interest groups. This opposition culminated in the National Unfunded Mandates (NUM) Day initiative, sponsored by the NLC, USCM, NACO, and International City/County Management Association. Held on October 27, 1993, local government officials across the nation held press conferences and public forums criticizing unfunded mandates, and released a study of the costs imposed by federal mandates on local governments. Over 300 cities and 128 counties participated in the study, which, when extrapolated nationally, estimated that federal mandates imposed additional costs of $6.5 billion annually for cities and $4.8 billion annually for counties.[150]

The NUM Day methodology used to estimate the costs of unfunded federal mandates was later challenged because of the absence of independent validation of local government submissions and the non-random nature of the participating jurisdictions. However, politically, NUM Day was considered a success by its organizers for two reasons. First, it attracted unprecedented media attention to the issue of unfunded federal mandates. For example, the number of newspaper articles discussing unfunded federal mandates increased from 22 in 1992, to 179 in 1993, and to 836 in 1994.[151] Second, it increased congressional awareness of state and local government concerns about unfunded mandates. For example, on January 5, 1995, Senator John Glenn mentioned NUM Day as having an impact on congressional awareness of unfunded mandates at a Senate congressional hearing on S. 1—The Unfunded Mandate Reform Act:

> On October 27, 1993, State and local elected officials from all over the Nation came to Washington and declared that day—"National Unfunded Mandates Day." These officials conveyed a powerful message to Congress and the Clinton Administration on the need for Federal mandate reform and relief. They raised four major objections to unfunded Federal mandates.
>
> First, unfunded Federal mandates impose unreasonable fiscal burdens on their budgets;
>
> Second, they limit State and local government flexibility to address more pressing local problems like crime and education;
>
> Third, Federal mandates too often come in a "one-size-fits-all" box that stifles the development of more innovative local efforts—efforts that ultimately may be more effective in solving the problem the Federal Mandate is meant to address; and

---

[149] Ibid., p. 42.

[150] Timothy J. Conlan, James D. Riggle, and Donna E. Schwartz, "Deregulating Federalism? The Politics of Mandate Reform in the 104th Congress," *Publius: The Journal of Federalism*, vol. 25, no. 3 (Summer 1995), p. 26; and Jeffrey L. Esser, "National Unfunded Mandates Day: An Idea Whose Time Has Come," *Government Finance Review*, vol. 9, no. 5 (October 1, 1993), p. 3, http://findarticles.com/p/articles/mi_hb6642/is_n5_v9/ai_n28629948/?tag=content.

[151] Timothy J. Conlan, James D. Riggle, and Donna E. Schwartz, "Deregulating Federalism? The Politics of Mandate Reform in the 104th Congress," *Publius: The Journal of Federalism*, vol. 25, no. 3 (Summer 1995), p. 27.

Fourth, they allow Congress to get credit for passing some worthy mandate or program, while leaving State and local governments with the difficult tasks of cutting services or raising taxes in order to pay for it.[152]

State and local government officials continued to lobby Congress for mandate relief legislation and coordinated their efforts to increase public awareness of their concerns. For example, on March 21, 1994, state and local government officials across the nation held town hall meetings and their affiliated public interest groups sponsored a rally on the Capitol steps to draw media attention to their concerns about unfunded federal mandates. The NLC and state municipal leagues across the country also declared October 24-30, 1994, Unfunded Mandates Week, which also generated considerable media coverage.[153]

The Initial Congressional Response

The efforts of state and local government officials appeared to have an effect on congressional legislative activity concerning unfunded federal mandates. During the 102nd Congress (1991-1992), 12 federal mandate relief bills were introduced in the House and 10 were introduced in the Senate. All of these bills failed to be reported out of committee, and only one had a congressional hearing. During the first session of the 103rd Congress (1993), 32 federal mandate relief bills were introduced and one of them, S. 993, the Federal Mandate Accountability and Reform Act of 1994 co-sponsored by Senators John Glenn and Dirk Kempthorne, was reported by the Senate Governmental Affairs Committee on June 16, 1994. It contained several provisions that were later in UMRA, and included an amendment offered by Senator Byron Dorgan "to include the private sector under the CBO and Committee mandate cost analysis requirements of Title I of S. 993, and a Glenn amendment to allow CBO to waive the private-sector cost analysis if CBO cannot make a "reasonable estimate" of the bills cost."[154] The bill was considered by the Senate on October 6, 1994, without a time agreement. After the introduction of several amendments and some debate, the Senate proceeded to other issues and adjourned without voting on the measure.[155] The House Government Operations Committee also reported a bill, H.R. 5128, the Federal Mandates Relief for State and Local Government Act of 1994, sponsored by Representative John Conyers, Jr., on October 5, 1994. It was similar to S. 993, but its approval was delayed, reportedly due to concerns raised by several senior Democratic Members worried that mandate legislation might make it more difficult to adopt laws to protect the environment and address social issues. Congress adjourned before the bill could move to the floor for consideration.[156]

---

[152] U.S. Congress, Senate Committee on Governmental Affairs, S. 1 - *Unfunded Mandates*, 104th Cong., 1st sess., January 5, 1995, S.Hrg. 104-392 (Washington: GPO, 1995), p. 5.

[153] Mary-Margaret Lamouth, "Local and Congressional Leaders Talk Mandates," *Nation's Cities Weekly*, March 21, 1994, p. 3; Beverly Schlotterbeck, "Rally to Stop the Mandate Madness Galvanizes Anti-mandate Campaign," *County News*, vol. 26, March 21, 1994, pp. 2, 3; and "Cities Gearing Up For National Unfunded Mandates Week," *Illinois Municipal Review* (September 1994), p. 13.

[154] U.S. Congress, Senate Committee on Governmental Affairs, *Unfunded Mandate Reform Act of 1995*, report to accompany S. 1, 104th Cong., 1st sess., January 11, 1995, S.Rept. 104-1 (Washington: GPO, 1995), p. 9.

[155] Ibid.

[156] Timothy J. Conlan, James D. Riggle, and Donna E. Schwartz, "Deregulating Federalism? The Politics of Mandate Reform in the 104th Congress," *Publius: The Journal of Federalism*, vol. 25, no. 3 (Summer 1995), pp. 28-31.

Core Federalism Principles Debated During UMRA's Consideration

The Republican Party gained control of the House of Representatives for the first time in 40 years following the congressional elections held on November 8, 1994. They also achieved a slim majority in the Senate as well.[157] Mandate reform was a key provision in the Republican Party's "Contract With America."[158] Perhaps reflecting its importance to the Republican leadership, the prospective Senate majority leader, Senator Robert Dole, designated a revised unfunded mandate relief bill, co-sponsored by Senators Kempthorne and Glenn and introduced on January 4, 1995, the opening day of the new Congress, as S. 1, the Unfunded Mandate Reform Act of 1995. The Senate Governmental Affairs Committee and Senate Budget Committee held a joint hearing on the bill the following day and it was reported out of the Senate Governmental Affairs Committee with three amendments (9 to 4) on January 9, 1995, and out of the Senate Budget Committee with four amendments (21-0) also on January 9, 1995.

To expedite Senate floor consideration, neither committee filed a committee report. Instead, the committee chairs, Senator William Roth, Jr. on behalf of the Senate Governmental Affairs Committee and Senator Pete Domenici on behalf of the Senate Budget Committee, each submitted a chairman's statement for insertion into the *Congressional Record*.[159] When Senate floor consideration commenced on January 12, 1995, Senator Robert Byrd objected to several features of the way the legislation was being handled, including the absence of a committee report and the pace of consideration. In addition, Senators introduced 228 amendments to the bill. Floor debate lasted for more than two weeks. During floor debate, Senator Kempthorne argued that the bill should be adopted out of a sense of fairness to state and local governments and as a commitment to federalism principles:

> Under this legislation, we are acknowledging for the first time, in a meaningful way, that there must be limits on the Federal Government's propensity to impose costly mandates on other levels of government. As the representatives of those governments have very effectively demonstrated, this is a real problem. Cities, for example, generally are fortunate if they have adequate resources just to meet their own local responsibilities. Unfunded Federal mandates have put a real strain on those resources. This has been the practice of the Federal Government for the past several decades, but in recent years it has mushroomed into an intolerable burden.
>
> This has been due, at least in part, to the Federal Government's own budget crisis. In the past, if Congress felt that a particular problem warranted a national solution, it would often

---

[157] Senator Richard Shelby of Alabama switched from the Democratic to the Republican Party on November 9, 1994, giving the Republican Party a majority of Senate seats.

[158] Representative Newt Gingrich, "Election of Speaker," remarks in the House, *Congressional Record*, vol. 141, part 1 (January 4, 1995), p. H444; Representative Dick Armey, "H. Res. 6, Title 1, Contract With America: A Bill of Accountability," House debate, *Congressional Record*, vol. 141, part 1 (January 4, 1995), pp. H662-H477; and U.S. Congress, House Committee on Ways and Means, *Contract With America - An Overview*, 104th Cong., 1st sess., January 5, 1995 (Washington: GPO, 1995), pp. 11-18.

[159] Senator William Roth, Jr., "Statement of the Chairman on the Reporting By the Governmental Affairs Committee of S. 1, Unfunded Mandate Reform Act of 1995," remarks in the Senate, *Congressional Record*, vol. 141, part 1 (January 9, 1995), pp. 891-898; and Senator Pete Domenici, "Statement of the Senate Committee on the Budget on S. 1, Unfunded Mandate Reform Act of 1995," remarks in the Senate, *Congressional Record*, vol. 141, part 1 (January 11, 1995), pp. 1092-1099.

fund that solution with Federal dollars. Mandates imposed on State and local governments could frequently be offset with generous Federal grants. But the Federal Government no longer has the money to fund the governmental actions it wishes to see accomplished throughout the country. In fact, it hasn't had the money to do this for many years. Instead, it borrowed for a long time, to cover those costs. But now the Federal deficit is so large, that the only alternative left for imposing so-called national solutions is to impose unfunded mandates....

The State legislators and Governors know this. This is why they feel so strongly that legislation regarding this practice must first be in place, before they are asked to ratify a balanced budget amendment. Otherwise, in the drive to achieve a balance Federal budget, Congress might be tempted to mandate that State and local governments shall pick up many of the costs that were formerly Federal. This is why any effort to add a sunset provision to this bill ought to be opposed. Our commitment to protect federalism ought to be permanent.

S. 1 is designed to put in place just such a mechanism. In this regard, it may truly be called balanced legislation. First of all, it helps bring our system of federalism back into balance, by serving as a check against the easy imposition of unfunded mandates. And, second, it does so in a way that strikes a balance between restraining the growth of mandates and recognizing that there may be legitimate exceptions.[160]

Senator Frank Lautenberg was among those opposing UMRA. He argued that the bill should be defeated because, among other things, the federal government has an obligation to set national standards to protect the environment and ensure the quality of life for all Americans:

Halting interstate pollution is an important responsibility of the Federal Government. And I am concerned that this act may have a chilling effect on future Federal environmental legislation. Another issue that may get loss in this debate is the benefit that States and their citizens derive from Federal mandates—even those not fully funded. States may say, we know how best to care for our citizens; a program that may be good for New Jersey, may not be good for Idaho or Ohio. But, I would argue that there is a broader national interest in some very fundamental issues which transcend that premise. I would argue that historically, not all States have provided a floor of satisfactory minimum decency standards for their citizens and that, as a democratic and fair society, we should worry about that. Further, as a practical matter, I would argue that the policies of one State in a society such as ours will certainly affect citizens and taxpayers of another State just as certainly as unfunded mandates can.

Let us look at our welfare system. There has been a lot of discussion about turning welfare over to the States, with few or virtually no Federal guidelines or requirements. What would happen if we do that? Would we see a movement of the disadvantaged between States, putting a heavier burden on the citizens of a State that provides more generous benefits?

Let us look at occupational safety, or environmental regulation. With a patchwork of differing standards across the States, would we see a migration of factories and jobs to States with lower standards? I think so. But by mandating floors in environmental and workplace conditions, the Federal Government ensures that States will comply with minimal standards befitting a complex, interrelated, and decent society.

---

[160] Senator Dirk Kempthorne, "Unfunded Mandate Reform Act," remarks in the Senate, *Congressional Record*, vol. 141, part 1 (January 12, 1995), p. 1166.

Or let us look at gun control. My State of New Jersey generally has strong controls on guns. But New Jerseyans still suffer from an epidemic of gun violence – in no small measure because firearms come into New Jersey from other States. Without strong national controls, this will remain a problem. That is why we passed a ban on all assault weapons and why we passed the Brady bill.

Currently the Federal Government discourages a scenario whereby a given State decides not to enforce some worker health and safety laws as a way of lowering costs and attracting industry. A State right next door might feel compelled to lower its standards in order to remain competitive. In the absence of a Federal Standard, we would likely see a bidding war that lowers the quality of life for all Americans.

These are some of a host of very fundamental, very basic, and even profound questions raised by the notion that we should never have unfunded mandates. These are questions each Member of the Senate should consider long and hard, before moving to drastically curtail— or make impossible—any unfunded mandates.[161]

After voting on 44 amendments and several cloture motions, the Senate approved S. 1 on January 27, 1995, 86-10.[162]

One of the amendments approved by the Senate was the "Byrd look-back amendment," which is the only provision in UMRA that allows for the regulation of any mandates based on actual rather than estimated costs.[163] It provided that legislation containing intergovernmental mandates would be considered funded, and hence not subject to a point of order, if it authorized appropriations to cover the estimated direct costs of the intergovernmental mandate and incorporated a prescribed mechanism requiring further review if, in any fiscal year, Congress did not appropriate funds sufficient to cover those costs. Under this mechanism, if the responsible federal agency determines that the appropriation provided was insufficient to cover the estimated direct costs of the mandate it shall notify the appropriate authorizing committees not later than 30 days after the start of the fiscal year and submit recommendations for either implementing a less costly mandate or making the mandate ineffective for the fiscal year. The statutory mechanism must also include expedited procedures for the consideration of legislative recommendations to achieve these outcomes not later than 30 days after the recommendations are submitted to Congress. Finally, the mechanism must provide that the mandate "shall be ineffective until such time as Congress has completed action on the recommendations of the responsible federal agency."[164] After Senator Robert Byrd offered this amendment, the Senate adopted it on January 26, 1995, 100-0.[165]

The House companion bill to S. 1 was H.R. 5, the Unfunded Mandate Reform Act of 1995, which was co-sponsored by Representatives William F. Clinger, Jr., Rob Portman, Gary A. Condit, and

---

[161] Senator Frank Lautenberg, "Unfunded Mandate Reform Act," remarks in the Senate, *Congressional Record*, vol. 141, part 1 (January 12, 1995), p. 1193.

[162] Timothy J. Conlan, James D. Riggle, and Donna E. Schwartz, "Deregulating Federalism? The Politics of Mandate Reform in the 104th Congress," *Publius: The Journal of Federalism*, vol. 25, no. 3 (Summer 1995), pp. 31, 32; and "Consideration of S. 1, Unfunded Mandate Reform Act, Senate Rollcall Vote No. 61," *Congressional Record*, vol. 141, part 2 (January 27, 1995), pp. 2750, 2751.

[163] Senator Robert Byrd, "Byrd Amendment No. 213," Amendments Submitted, Unfunded Mandate Reform Act of 1995," *Congressional Record*, vol. 141, part 2 (January 24, 1995), p. 2195. See 2 U.S.C. §658d(a)(B).

[164] Ibid.

[165] "Consideration of S. 1, Unfunded Mandate Reform Act, Senate Rollcall Vote No. 49," *Congressional Record*, vol. 141, part 2 (January 26, 1995), pp. 2606, 2607.

Thomas M. Davis. It was reported by the House Government Reform and Oversight Committee, on January 13, 1995, by voice vote and without hearings.[166] Floor consideration began on January 20, 1995. Numerous amendments were introduced by Democratic Members to add various exemptions to the bill, such as the health of children and the disabled, the disposal of nuclear waste, and child support enforcement. These amendments were rejected on party-line votes. On February 1, 1995, H.R. 5 was adopted, 360-74, inserted into S. 1 as a House substitute, and sent to conference.[167]

There were two major differences between the House and Senate versions of S. 1. The House version did not include the Byrd look-back amendment, and it permitted judicial review of federal agency compliance with the bill's provisions. Initially, House conferees refused to accept the Byrd look-back amendment and Senate conferees, worried that outside parties could delay regulations for years by filing lawsuits, refused to accept judicial review of federal agency compliance with the bill's provisions. Negotiations continued for six weeks. The deadlock over judicial review was ended by allowing judicial review of whether an appropriate analysis of mandate costs was done, but restricting the court's ability to second-guess the quality of the cost estimates. The deadlock over the Byrd look-back amendment ended when House conferees accepted its inclusion after being assured that its intent was to make certain that Congress, rather than an executive agency, retained responsibility for setting policy.[168]

The Senate adopted the conference report, which renamed the bill the Unfunded Mandates Reform Act of 1995, on March 15, 1995, 91-9, and the House adopted it the next day, 394-28. President Bill Clinton signed it on March 22, 1995.[169]

---

[166] Representative William F. Clinger, Jr., Chair of the House Government Reform and Oversight Committee, indicated in the committee's report that hearings were not necessary because "the Committee held several hearings on this issue as well as on a similar bill last session." Members from the minority party argued in the committee's report that "The haste in which this bill was considered left a number of substantive issues unaddressed, which even the authors conceded at markup that they would like to address on the Floor. Most importantly, a ruling from the Chairman in the middle of the markup prohibited members from offering amendments to the operative sections of Title II and III." U.S. Congress, House Committee on Government Reform and Oversight, *Unfunded Mandate Reform Act of 1995*, report to accompany H.R. 5, 104th Cong., 1st sess., January 13, 1995, H.Rept. 104-1, Part 2 (Washington: GPO, 1995), pp. 53-56. Portions of the bill were also sequentially referred to and reported by the Committees on Rules, Budget, and Judiciary.

[167] "Consideration of H.R. 5, Unfunded Mandate Reform Act, House Roll No. 83," *Congressional Record*, vol. 141, part 3 (February 1, 1995), p. 3252, 3258; and Timothy J. Conlan, James D. Riggle, and Donna E. Schwartz, "Deregulating Federalism? The Politics of Mandate Reform in the 104th Congress," *Publius: The Journal of Federalism*, vol. 25, no. 3 (Summer 1995), pp. 33, 34.

[168] Timothy J. Conlan, James D. Riggle, and Donna E. Schwartz, "Deregulating Federalism? The Politics of Mandate Reform in the 104th Congress," *Publius: The Journal of Federalism*, vol. 25, no. 3 (Summer 1995), pp. 36, 37.

[169] "Unfunded Mandate Reform Act of 1995 – Conference Report, Senate Rollcall Vote No. 104," *Congressional Record*, vol. 141, part 6 (March 15, 1995), p. 7876; "Conference Report on S. 1, Unfunded Mandate Reform Act, House Roll No. 252," *Congressional Record*, vol. 141, part 6 (March 16, 1995), p. 8136; and President Bill Clinton, "Remarks on Signing the Unfunded Mandates Reform Act of 1995," *Weekly Compilation of Presidential Documents*, vol. 31, no. 12 (March 22, 1995), pp. 453-455.

Appendix B. UMRA Points of Order

1. Rep. Bill Archer, "Contract With America Advancement Act of 1996," House debate on motion to recommit H.R. 3136, *Congressional Record*, vol. 142, part 5 (March 28, 1996), pp. 6931-6937.

2. Rep. Rob Portman, "The Employee Commuting Act of 1996," House debate on H.R. 1227, *Congressional Record*, vol. 142, part 9 (May 23, 1996), pp. 12283-12287.

3. Rep. Bill Orton, "The Welfare – Medicaid Reform Act of 1996," House debate on H.R. 3734, *Congressional Record*, vol. 142, part 13 (July 18, 1996), p. 17668.

4. Rep. Melvin Watt, "The Housing Opportunity and Responsibility Act," House debate on H.R. 2, *Congressional Record*, vol. 143, part 5 (May 1, 1997), pp. 7006-7012.

5. Rep. John Ensign, "The Nuclear Waste Policy Act of 1997," House debate on H.R, 1270, *Congressional Record*, vol. 143, no, 148 (October 29, 1997), pp. H9655-H9657.

6. Rep. Gerald Soloman, "The Agricultural Research, Extension, and Education Reform Act of 1998," House debate on the conference report for S. 1150, *Congressional Record*, vol. 144, part 8 (June 4, 1998), pp. H9655-H9657.

7. Rep. Jerrold Nadler, "The Bankruptcy Reform Act of 1998," House debate on H.R. 3150, *Congressional Record*, vol. 144, part 8 (June 10, 1998), pp. 11853-11857.

8. Rep. Steve Largent, "The Minimum Wage Increase Act," House debate on H.R. 3846, *Congressional Record*, vol. 144, part 2 (March 9, 2000), pp. 2623-2624.

9. Rep. James Gibbons, "The Nuclear Waste Policy Amendments Act of 2000," House debate on S. 1287, *Congressional Record*, vol. 146, part 2 (March 22, 2000), pp. 3234-3236.

10. Rep. John Conyers, "The Internet Nondiscrimination Act of 2000," House debate on H.R. 3709, *Congressional Record*, vol. 146, part 6 (May 10, 2000), pp. 7483-7485.

11. Rep. Charles Stenholm, "The Medicare RX 2000 Act," House debate on H.R. 4680, *Congressional Record*, vol. 146, part 9 (June 28, 2000), pp. 12650-12653.

12. Rep. Jim Moran, "The Department of Transportation Appropriations Act, 2002," House debate on H.R. 2299, *Congressional Record*, vol. 147, part 9 (June 26, 2001), pp. 11906-11910.

13. Rep. James Gibbons, "The Yucca Mountain Repository Site Approval Act," House debate on H.J.Res. 87, *Congressional Record*, vol. 148, part 5 (May 8, 2002), pp. 7145-7148.

14. Rep. Sheila Jackson-Lee, "The Real ID Act of 2005," House debate on H.R. 418, *Congressional Record*, vol. 151, no. 13 (February 9, 2005), pp. H437-H442.

15. Rep. James McGovern, "The Energy Policy Act of 2005," House debate on H.R. 6, *Congressional Record*, vol. 151, no. 48 (April 20, 2005), pp. H2174-H2178.

16. Sen. Kit Bond, "The Transportation, Treasury, HUD and Independent Agencies Appropriations Act, 2006," Senate debate on H.R. 3058, *Congressional Record*, vol. 151, no. 133 (October 19, 2005), p. S11547.

17. Sen. Ted Kennedy, "The Transportation, Treasury, HUD and Independent Agencies Appropriations Act, 2006," Senate debate on H.R. 3058, *Congressional Record*, vol. 151, no. 133 (October 19, 2005), p. S11548.

18. Rep. Jim McDermott, "The Deficit Reduction Act of 2005," House debate on H.R. 4241, *Congressional Record*, vol. 151, no. 152 (November 17, 2005), pp. H10531-H10534.

19. Rep. Jim McDermott, "The Deficit Reduction Act of 2005," House debate on H.Res. 653, *Congressional Record*, vol. 152, no. 10 (February 1, 2006), pp. H37-H40.

20. Rep. Tammy Baldwin, "The Communications Opportunity, Promotion, and Enhancement Act of 2006," House debate on H.R. 5252, *Congressional Record*, vol. 152, no. 72 (June 8, 2006), pp. H3506-H3510.

21. Rep. Jim McDermott, "The Federal Election Integrity Act of 2006," House debate on H.R. 4844, *Congressional Record*, vol. 152, no. 118 (September 20, 2006), pp. H6742-H6745.

22. Rep. Pete Sessions, "The Children's Health and Medicare Protections Act of 2007," House debate on H.R. 3162, *Congressional Record*, vol. 153, no. 124-125 (August 1, 2007), pp. H9288-H9290.

23. Rep. Pete Sessions, "The Children's Health Insurance Program Reauthorization Act of 2007," House debate on H.R. 3963, *Congressional Record*, vol. 153, no. 163 (October 25, 2007), pp. H12027-H12029.

24. Rep. Jeff Flake, "Senate Amendments to H.R. 6, Energy Independence and Security Act of 2007," House debate on H.R. 6, *Congressional Record*, vol. 153, no. 186 (December 6, 2007), pp. H4255-H4259.

25. Rep. Mike Conaway, "The Renewable Energy and Energy Conservation Tax Act of 2008," House debate on H.R. 5351, *Congressional Record*, vol. 154, no. 32 (February 27, 2008), pp. H1079-H1082.

26. Rep. Paul Broun, "The Paul Wellstone Mental Health and Addiction Equity Act of 2007," House debate on H.R. 1424, *Congressional Record*, vol. 154, no. 37 (March 5, 2008), pp. H1259-H1262.

27. Rep. Jeff Flake, "The Food, Conservation, and Energy Act of 2008," House debate on H.R. 2419, *Congressional Record*, vol. 154, no. 79 (May 14, 2008), pp. H3784-H3789.

28. Rep. Eric Cantor, "The Comprehensive American Energy Security and Consumer Protection Act," House debate on H.R. 6899, *Congressional Record*, vol. 154, no. 147 (September 16, 2008), pp. H8152-H8157.

29. Rep. Jeff Flake, "The Consolidated Security, Disaster Assistance and Continuing Appropriations Act, 2009," House debate on H.R. 2638, *Congressional Record*, vol. 154, no. 152 (September 24, 2008), pp. H9218-H9220.

30. Rep. David Drier, "The American Recovery and Reinvestment Act," House debate on H.R. 1, *Congressional Record*, vol. 155, no. 30 (February 13, 2009), pp. H1524-H1536.

31. Rep. Jeff Flake, "The Omnibus Appropriations Act, 2009," House debate on H.R. 1105, *Congressional Record*, vol. 155, no. 33 (February 25, 2009), pp. H2643-H2646.

32. Rep. Jeff Flake, "The Agriculture, Rural Development, Food and Drug Administration Appropriations Act, 2010," House debate on H.R. 2997, *Congressional Record*, vol. 155, no. 101 (July 8, 2009), pp. H7783-H7786.

33. Rep. Jeff Flake, "The Military Construction and Veteran's Affairs Appropriations Act, 2010," House debate on H.R. 3082, *Congressional Record*, vol. 155, no. 103 (July 10, 2009), pp. H7951-H7953.

34. Rep. Jeff Flake, "The Energy and Water Development Appropriations Act, 2010," House debate on H.R. 3183, *Congressional Record*, vol. 155, no. 106 (July 15, 2009), pp. H8107-H8109.

35. Rep. Jeff Flake, "The Financial Services and General Government Appropriations Act, 2010," House debate on H.R. 3170, *Congressional Record*, vol. 155, no. 107 (July 16, 2009), pp. H8191-H8193.

36. Rep. Jeff Flake, "The Transportation, Housing and Urban Development Appropriations Act, 2010," House debate on H.R. 3288, *Congressional Record*, vol. 155, no. 112 (July 23, 2009), pp. H8593-H8594.

37. Rep. Jeff Flake, "The Departments of Labor, Health, and Human Services, and Education Appropriations Act, 2010," House debate on H.R. 3293, *Congressional Record*, vol. 155, no. 113 (July 24, 2009), pp. H8593-H8594.

38. Rep. Jeff Flake, "The Department of Defense Appropriations Act, 2010," House debate on H.R. 3326, *Congressional Record*, vol. 155, no. 116 (July 29, 2009), pp. H8977-H8978.

39. Senator Robert Corker, "H.R. 3590, the Service Members Home Ownership Act of 2009," remarks in the Senate, *Congressional Record*, daily edition, vol. 155, no. 199 (December 23, 2009), pp. S13803- S13804.

40. Rep. Paul Ryan, "Providing for Consideration of Senate Amendments to H.R. 3590, Service Members Home Ownership Tax Act of 2009, and Providing for Consideration of H.R. 4872, Health Care and Education Reconciliation Act of 2010," House debate on H.Res. 1203, *Congressional Record*, daily edition, vol. 156, no. 43 (March 21, 2010), pp. H1825-H1828.

41. Rep. Jeff Flake, "Providing For Consideration of H.R. 5822, Military Construction and Veterans Affairs and Related Agencies Appropriations Act, 2011," House debate on H.R. 5822, *Congressional Record*, vol. 156, no. 112 (July 28, 2010), pp. H6206-H6209.

42. Rep. Jeff Flake, "Providing For Consideration of H.R. 5850, Transportation, Housing And Urban Development, and Related Agencies Appropriations Act, 2011," House debate on H.R. 5850, *Congressional Record*, vol. 156, no. 113 (July 29, 2010), pp. H6298-H6290.

43. Rep. Jeff Flake, "Providing For Consideration of Senate Amendment to House Amendment to Senate Amendment to H.R. 4853, Tax Relief, Unemployment Insurance Reauthorization, and Job Creation Act of 2010," House debate on H.R. 4853, *Congressional Record*, vol. 156, no. 157 (December 16, 2010), pp. H8525-H8526.

44. Rep. Keith Ellison, "Providing For Consideration of H.R. 1255, Government Shutdown Prevention Act of 2011," House debate on H.Res. 194, *Congressional Record*, vol. 157, no. 46 (April 1, 2011), pp. H2219-H2222.

45. Rep. John Garamendi, "Providing For Further Consideration of H.R. 1540, National Defense Authorization Act for Fiscal Year 2012," House debate on H.Res. 276, *Congressional Record*, vol. 157, no. 73 (May 25, 2011), pp. H3423-H3424.

46. Rep. Keith Ellison, "Providing For Consideration of H.R. 2017, Department of Homeland Security Appropriations Act, 2012," House debate on H.Res. 287, *Congressional Record*, vol. 157, no. 77 (June 1, 2011), pp. H3816-H3818.

47. Rep. John Garamendi, "Providing For Further Consideration of H.R. 2021, Jobs and Energy Permitting Act of 2011 and Providing for Consideration of H.R. 1249, America Invents Act," House debate on H.Res. 316, *Congressional Record*, vol. 157, no. 73 (June 22, 2011), pp. H4379-H.4380.

48. Rep. Marcia Fudge, "Providing For Consideration of H.R. 1315, Consumer Financial Protection Safety and Soundness Improvement Act of 2011," House debate on H.Res. 358, *Congressional Record*, vol. 157, no. 110 (July 21, 2011), p. H5302.

49. Rep. Gwen Moore, "Providing For Consideration of H.R. 358, Protect Life Act," House debate on H.Res. 430, *Congressional Record*, vol. 157, no. 153 (October 13, 2011), pp. H6869, H6870.

50. Rep. Gwen Moore, "Providing For Consideration of H.R. 3630: Middle Class Tax Relief and Job Creation Act of 2011," House debate on H.Res. 491, *Congressional Record*, vol. 157, no. 191 (December 13, 2011), pp. H8745-H8748.

51. Rep. Gwen Moore, "Providing For Consideration of H.R. 4089: Sportsmen's Heritage Act of 2012, and for Other Purposes," House debate on H.Res. 614, *Congressional Record*, vol. 158, no. 55 (April 17, 2012), pp. H1860-H1862.

52. Rep. Gwen Moore, "Providing For Consideration of H.R. 4970, the Violence Against Women Reauthorization Act of 2012, and Providing For Consideration of H.R. 4310, the National Defense Authorization Act for Fiscal Year 2013," House debate on H.Res. 656, *Congressional Record*, vol. 158, no. 70 (May 16, 2012), pp. H2776-H2731.

53. Rep. Gwen Moore, "Providing For Consideration of House Joint Resolution 118, Disapproving Rule Relating To Waiver and Expenditure Authority with Respect to the Temporary Assistance For Needy Families Program. Providing For Consideration of H.R. 3409, the Stop The War On Coal Act of 2012; and Providing For Proceedings during the Period from September 22, 2012, through November 12, 2012," House debate on H.Res. 788, *Congressional Record*, vol. 158, no. 128 (September 20, 2012), pp. H6165-H6173.

Author Contact Information

Robert Jay Dilger
Senior Specialist in American National Government
rdilger@crs.loc.gov, 7-3110

Richard S. Beth
Specialist on Congress and the Legislative Process
rbeth@crs.loc.gov, 7-8667